Costa Rica Guide 2025-2026.

Step-by-step itineraries, insider tips, hidden gems, eco adventures, maps, culture, wildlife, and budget-friendly explorations

Betty G. Coffman

Copyright © 2025

All rights reserved. No part of this publication may be reproduced, distributed, or transmitted in any form or by any means, including photocopying, recording, or other electronic or mechanical methods, without the prior written permission of the publisher, except for brief quotations in critical reviews and certain other noncommercial uses permitted by copyright law.

This book is a non-fiction work. All characters, incidents, and dialogue are based on the author personal experiences, interviews, and research. Any resemblance to actual persons, living or dead, or events is purely coincidental.

While every effort has been made to provide accurate and up-to-date information, neither the author nor the publisher can be held liable for any errors or omissions or for any consequences resulting from the use of this information

Table of Contents

Introduction 8
   Welcome to Costa Rica: The Jewel of Central America 8
   How to Use This Guide: Insider Tips & Reader Tools 9
   What's New in 2025–2026 10
   Must-Know Travel Facts & Local Etiquette 11

Part 1: Planning Your Perfect Trip 13

Chapter 1: Costa Rica at a Glance 14
   1.1 Quick Facts & Stats (Expanded Through Narrative) 15
   1.2 Regional Breakdown: Coasts, Highlands, and Rainforests (Continued) 17
   1.3 Weather by Region and Season (Expanded) .. 18
   1.4 Currency, Visas, and Vaccines (Expanded) 20

Chapter 2: When to Go & Where to Start 22
   2.1 Best Times to Visit (Month-by-Month Breakdown) 22
   2.2 Custom Itineraries 25
      2.2.1 7 Days in Costa Rica (Highlights Only) ... 26
      2.2.2 14-Day Explorer's Journey 26
      2.2.3 Family Adventure Route 28
      2.2.4 Romantic Getaway Itinerary 29
      2.2.5 Backpacker's Budget Trail 30

2.3 Packing Smart for the Tropics........................31

Chapter 3: Getting In & Around 33

    3.1 Airports & Entry Points....................................33

    3.2 Local Transport: Planes, Buses, Shuttles, Boats 35

    3.3 Renting a Car in Costa Rica: Tips & Warnings 36

    3.4 Road Conditions, GPS Apps & Signage 37

Part 2: Destination Deep Dive – Region by Region..39

Chapter 4: San José & Central Valley 40

    4.1 Must-See: National Theatre, Gold & Jade Museums 41

    4.2 Nightlife, Cafés & Urban Culture.....................44

    4.3 Where to Stay: From Boutique to Budget 45

    4.4 Day Trips: Poás Volcano, Coffee Farms & Waterfalls...48

Chapter 5: Alajuela & Around 54

    5.1 Gateway to Adventure: La Paz Gardens & Poás Volcano..55

    5.2 Coffee Routes & Plantation Tours 56

    5.3 Local Eats & Traditional Dishes 58

    5.4 Practical Travel Tips for Exploring Alajuela 61

Chapter 6: Cartago & Orosi Valley 64

    6.1 Spiritual and Scenic: Basilica de Los Ángeles 65

    6.2 Irazú Volcano & Hidden Thermal Springs 66

6.3 Best Boutique Hotels & Wellness Escapes (With Cost Breakdown) 69

Chapter 7: Heredia 73

7.1 Cultural Hotspot Near the Capital 73

7.2 Traditional Markets, Food Tours & Artisan Stops 75

7.3 Best Eats on a Budget 77

Chapter 8: Limón & the Caribbean Coast 82

8.1 Afro-Caribbean Flavor & Rhythms 83

8.2 Tortuguero & Cahuita National Parks 84

8.3 Wildlife Watching & Coastal Relaxation 86

8.4 Caribbean Cuisine & Beachfront Lodges 88

Chapter 9 Puntarenas & Nicoya Peninsula 93

9.1 Monteverde Cloud Forest 93

9.2 Surf Towns — Santa Teresa, Mal País, Montezuma 100

9.3 Wellness Resorts & Yoga Retreats 107

Chapter 10: Guanacaste – Pacific Dreams and Volcanic Wilds 114

10.1 Beach Escapes: Tamarindo, Playa Flamingo, Playa Conchal 115

10.2 Eco-Luxury Stays & Sunset Spots 117

10.3 Rincón de la Vieja Adventures 121

10.4 Beyond the Beaches: Inland Towns, Culture, and the Soul of Guanacaste 127

Part 3: Themed Experiences & Insider Guides 132

Chapter 11: Adventure & Nature..............................133

    11.1 Hiking, Ziplining & Caving Hotspots 133

    11.2 Best National Parks for Wildlife Viewing 138

    11.3 Water Adventures: Surfing, Rafting, Snorkeling, Scuba...142

Chapter 12: Eco-Tourism & Sustainability 148

    12.1 What Makes Costa Rica a Global Leader...148

    12.2 Top Eco-Lodges & Sustainable Tours 150

    12.3 How to Travel Responsibly 151

Chapter 13 Culture & Cuisine..............................153

    13.1: Local Dishes to Try & Where to Find Them 153

    13.2: Food Markets & Street Eats.......................158

    13.3: Festivals to Catch in 2025–2026................162

    13.4: Cooking Classes & Cultural Workshops 168

Chapter 14: Digital Nomads & Remote Workers 172

    14.1 Best Places to Live & Work.........................173

    14.2 Internet Access & Coworking Spots............175

    14.3 Budgeting a Remote Life in Paradise 176

    14.4 Community Events & Meetups....................179

Chapter 15: Family-Friendly Costa Rica............181

    15.1 Kid-Friendly Activities by Region.................181

    15.2 Wildlife Encounters & Educational Fun.......183

    15.3 Best Family Resorts & Safe Beaches 184

Part 4: Practical Traveler Toolkit 186

Chapter 16: Budgeting & Money-Saving Tips 187

    16.1 Hidden Costs to Watch 187

    16.2 Where to Eat, Stay & Play on a Budget 191

    16.3 Sample Daily Budgets for All Traveler Types 194

Chapter 17: Health, Safety & Travel Insurance 199

    17.1 Common Illnesses & How to Avoid Them ... 199

    17.2 Staying Safe in Urban vs Rural Areas 202

Chapter 18: Spanish Phrases for Travelers 205

    18.1 Essential Words & Phrases 206

    18.2 Restaurant, Market, & Taxi Language 207

    18.3 Fun Local Slang (Tico-isms!) 208

Map 210

Introduction

"In Costa Rica, we don't say hello — we say 'Pura Vida.' It means pure life, but it really means everything."

Welcome to Costa Rica: The Jewel of Central America

If you were to ask ten travelers what they remember most about Costa Rica, you'd get ten different answers — but they'd all be told with a spark in the eye. Some would speak of waking up to the sound of howler monkeys in the jungle canopy. Others would describe the rush of catching their first Pacific wave, or the unexpected peace of sipping freshly brewed coffee in a quiet mountain village. And then there are those who'll simply say: "It changed me."

Costa Rica is not just another destination — it's a living, breathing encounter with nature, culture, and self. Nestled between the Pacific Ocean and Caribbean Sea, this small Central American nation offers more than its modest size suggests. With over 25% of its land protected in national parks and reserves, it is a model for biodiversity conservation. Costa Rica is home to over **5% of the world's species**, despite occupying less than 0.05% of the planet's surface. That kind of statistic isn't just impressive — it sets the tone for the kind of journey you're about to take.

This guide has been written with a simple promise: to help you experience Costa Rica fully — not just see it, but *feel* it, *understand* it, and *carry it with you*. Whether you're a first-time visitor or a returning explorer, the country will never greet you the same way twice.

How to Use This Guide: Insider Tips & Reader Tools

This book is more than just a travel manual — it's a curated companion designed for **modern travelers with diverse goals**. Some of you are here for eco-retreats and wellness. Others may be planning the ultimate digital nomad escape or a family trip with curious young explorers in tow. Regardless of your reason, this guide adapts to your journey.

Each regional chapter covers not just what to see, but *why* you should care. Attractions are filtered through experience — not just "places on a map," but recommendations grounded in value, uniqueness, and practical impact. For every town or region, you'll find lodging options sorted by budget and vibe, from treehouse hotels to beachside hostels. Dining sections don't just name-drop restaurants; they give you a taste of what locals are ordering, what you can't miss, and how to spot a tourist trap.

In the themed chapters — like **eco-tourism, digital nomad life, adventure travel**, or **family-friendly destinations** — you'll find deeper insights tailored to your specific interests. These aren't afterthoughts — they reflect the real ways people experience Costa Rica today.

To keep up with changing travel trends and 2025–2026 realities, the guide also references *digital tools*, mobile apps, and QR code-accessed bonuses where applicable. These might link to updated maps, bus schedules, or exclusive discounts with eco-lodges or local guides (especially valuable for readers using Kindle or an interactive PDF).

You'll also find local voices sprinkled throughout — real quotes from guides, business owners, or seasoned travelers. Costa Rica is a place best learned through stories, and this book honors that spirit

What's New in 2025–2026

If you've visited Costa Rica before, you'll notice that 2025 has brought subtle yet significant changes. A global spotlight on sustainable tourism has intensified, and Costa Rica remains a leader — but the government has tightened regulations on park entry, trail limits, and drone use. Several parks, including **Tortuguero** and **Corcovado**, now require advance bookings through a centralized system. Don't assume you can "just show up" anymore.

Infrastructure is also evolving. The highway connecting San José to the Caribbean coast has undergone major upgrades, cutting travel time dramatically — a game-changer for those planning a loop through Limón and back. More eco-lodges in remote regions are offering **solar-powered co-working spaces**, attracting digital nomads and remote professionals in greater numbers than ever before.

Cultural tourism has expanded too. Towns like **Puerto Viejo** and **Monteverde** are hosting new festivals, artisan markets, and community experiences supported by sustainable tourism initiatives. In 2026, Costa Rica will host its **first National Indigenous Culture Month**, bringing renewed attention to the country's Bribri, Cabécar, and Maleku communities — offering opportunities for respectful, immersive travel.

Health protocols post-2020s pandemic years have largely relaxed, but some wildlife sanctuaries and indigenous areas still enforce strict guidelines, particularly when it comes to contact and cleanliness. Don't be surprised if hand-washing and shoe-sanitizing stations are part of your jungle trek experience.

Must-Know Travel Facts & Local Etiquette

Costa Rica is one of the safest countries in Latin America, but that doesn't mean you can throw caution to the wind. Petty theft in tourist zones still occurs — especially in crowded areas like San José's central market or the Pacific beach towns during peak season. Travelers are advised to use hotel safes, avoid flashing valuables, and be extra cautious at night in urban areas.

Tipping is customary but not obligatory; most restaurants already include a 10% service charge in the bill. Still, an extra tip is always appreciated — especially by guides, drivers, and housekeepers who often go the extra mile.

You'll hear the phrase **"Pura Vida"** everywhere. It means more than "pure life." It's a greeting, a thank you, a way to say all is well, even when it's not. It reflects a national mindset — one of resilience, kindness, and flow. Respond with a smile, and you'll earn the warmth of a culture that values friendliness over formality.

Dress codes are relaxed almost everywhere, but when visiting churches or rural communities, modesty is respected. Learn a few Spanish basics — not because it's required, but because it shows respect. A simple *"Buenos días"* goes a long way in a country where human connection is prized.

Costa Rica uses the **Costa Rican colón**, though U.S. dollars are accepted in most tourist zones. ATMs are widely available, especially in cities and coastal towns. Avoid currency exchange booths at airports — they often have the worst rates. Instead, use your debit card or withdraw cash once you're in town.

Finally, remember: Costa Rica isn't a checklist country. You're not here to race from one attraction to the next. The beauty lies in **slowing down**, in **staying longer in one place**, in letting conversations and sunsets unfold without pressure.

ai
Part 1: Planning Your Perfect Trip

Chapter 1: Costa Rica at a Glance

"In Costa Rica, we don't just live — we feel. We greet the sunrise with birdsong, measure time in sunsets, and believe that the happiest life is the simplest one." — **local proverb overheard in a San Ramón café.**

Costa Rica is not a place you visit. It's a place you absorb. It stays on your skin like sea salt and seeps into your thoughts like the sound of cicadas at dusk. Before you dive into its cities, volcanoes, or jungles, you need a working sense of what this small but mighty nation is all about. Not in vague poetic terms, but in grounded, useful, need-to-know details that will make your trip smarter, smoother, and significantly more rewarding.

Roughly the size of West Virginia or Denmark, Costa Rica punches well above its weight in natural diversity, ecological significance, and tourism value. With just over 5 million residents — about the same population as Minnesota — this Central American nation manages to protect more than **25% of its landmass** as national parks, biological reserves, and wildlife refuges. That's more than nearly any country on Earth. This isn't by accident. Costa Rica has become an intentional sanctuary for nature and a leading global model for eco-conscious living.

It's no wonder that it's a favorite for travelers ranging from surfers and backpackers to retirees and remote-working software engineers. Yet what makes it shine isn't just the sloths or the surf breaks. It's the balance — the way modern, safe infrastructure meets wild, untamed nature. You can leave a luxury boutique hotel in the morning and be hiking through a cloud forest by lunch. You can sip third-wave coffee roasted on-site in the Central Valley while watching toucans glide overhead. This is a country designed to surprise you — subtly, constantly, and with a rare sense of sincerity.

1.1 Quick Facts & Stats (Expanded Through Narrative)

Costa Rica is a country that refuses to be summed up by numbers, but some figures still tell an impressive story. The country boasts more than **500,000 species** — nearly **5% of the world's biodiversity** — packed into less than **0.03% of the planet's landmass**. That's not a typo. This makes Costa Rica one of the most biologically intense places on Earth, a label earned not through tourism campaigns, but through decades of conservation science and real government commitment to the environment.

The official language is **Spanish**, but in hotels, popular attractions, and urban zones, you'll find English widely spoken — and increasingly, menus and signage accommodate both languages. Still, a few key Spanish phrases will earn you respect, especially in rural areas. The locals, affectionately known as **Ticos** (men) and **Ticas** (women), are famously warm and patient with travelers, especially those who make even a small effort to speak the language.

Costa Rica's political structure is democratic and stable, with **no military** — a rarity in Latin America. This isn't just an interesting fact; it's part of the country's identity. Since abolishing its armed forces in 1949, Costa Rica has invested heavily in public health, education, and environmental protections. As a result, the country ranks consistently high on global happiness and life satisfaction indexes, and travelers often remark on the relaxed but purposeful energy that characterizes daily life here.

Internet penetration is excellent — over **80%** nationwide — and mobile coverage reaches even some remote corners. This makes it an ideal destination not just for traditional tourists, but for digital nomads, remote workers, and content creators looking for both inspiration and connectivity.

1.2 Regional Breakdown: Coasts, Highlands, and Rainforests (Continued)

To understand Costa Rica is to understand its **geographic split** — not just the formal provinces, but the functional travel regions that shape your experience of the country. Though it takes just a few hours to drive coast to coast, the shift in atmosphere, culture, and environment between regions is stark and immediate.

The **Northern Pacific**, largely synonymous with **Guanacaste Province**, is known for its dry climate and miles of beach. This is where many first-time visitors land, thanks to the **Daniel Oduber Quirós International Airport** in Liberia. Expect modern beach towns, surfing schools, yoga retreats, and high-end resorts — alongside stretches of beach that remain blissfully undeveloped.

Move south along the **Nicoya Peninsula**, and you enter the realm of the slow traveler. Places like **Nosara**, **Samara**, and **Santa Teresa** attract wellness seekers, digital nomads, and off-grid dreamers. The roads here are rougher, the sunsets louder, and the pace of life genuinely slower.

The **Central Pacific**, home to **Jacó**, **Manuel Antonio**, and **Dominical**, is a study in contrast. You'll find nightlife and casinos rubbing shoulders with family-friendly national parks, scenic waterfalls, and boutique hideaways perched above the cliffs.

Then there's the **South Pacific** and **Osa Peninsula**, considered Costa Rica's final frontier. This region is rugged, remote, and wild — a place where scarlet macaws outnumber people and jungle lodges replace traditional hotels. For those serious about wildlife, this is where the real treasure lies.

The **Caribbean Coast**, meanwhile, has its own rhythm. The port city of **Limón** may not charm at first glance, but the southern towns of **Cahuita**, **Puerto Viejo**, and **Manzanillo** offer a mix of Afro-Caribbean culture, reggae-infused beach towns, and jungle-lined coastlines. The food is different here, as is the music, the dialect, and even the sense of time.

Inland, the **Central Highlands** rise dramatically, anchored by the urban sprawl of **San José** but extending into coffee country, artisan villages, and cooler elevations. Towns like **Grecia**, **Atenas**, and **Sarchí** are havens for expats, thanks to their mild climate and tight-knit communities. Meanwhile, **Monteverde**, high in the Tilarán Mountains, is the poster child for cloud forests — where moss hangs from the branches and howler monkeys wake you before dawn.

The **Northern Lowlands**, home to **La Fortuna** and **Arenal Volcano**, blend geothermal wonder with adrenaline. Zip-lining, whitewater rafting, and hot spring soaking can all happen within a single day. It's where Costa Rica's tourist industry first found its footing — and where it still dazzles.

1.3 Weather by Region and Season (Expanded)

Costa Rica's climate isn't defined by four seasons, but by two: dry and wet. Yet this binary is misleading. What you actually get is a country of **microclimates**, each with its own personality.

In the **dry season**, which typically spans **December through April**, skies are clear and travel conditions are ideal. It's peak tourist season — and with good reason. This is when the **Pacific Coast** truly shines. Beaches are sun-drenched, trails are firm, and most attractions operate at full capacity. But it's also the most expensive time to visit, with higher prices for flights and accommodations.

Come **May**, the landscape changes. The **green season** begins — a misnomer that turns off some travelers but charms many others. Rain usually falls in the late afternoon, leaving mornings clear and fresh. Rivers swell, forests flourish, and the tourist crowds thin out. Photographers and nature lovers often prefer this season, especially in **June and July**, when there's typically a mini-dry spell known locally as *veranillo de San Juan*.

From **September to November**, rainfall intensifies, especially in the Pacific zones. Some remote lodges shut down, roads in certain areas become impassable, and the country seems to take a collective breath. Yet this is when the **Caribbean Coast** enjoys its sunniest, driest days — a geographic paradox that rewards those who understand Costa Rica's nuanced weather dance.

Temperature-wise, the **coastal lowlands** stay hot year-round, often climbing into the high 80s and low 90s Fahrenheit (30–34°C). The **central valley and highlands** are much cooler, with daytime highs in the 70s (21–25°C) and crisp nights. Elevation, more than season, dictates how warm or cool you'll feel in any given place.

1.4 Currency, Visas, and Vaccines (Expanded)

The Costa Rican **colón** is colorful, durable, and increasingly digital. Though U.S. dollars are widely accepted in tourist areas, paying in colones often gets you a better rate, especially at local shops, gas stations, and markets. As of early 2025, **1 USD equals around 530–550 CRC**, but exchange rates can shift slightly week to week.

ATMs are reliable and found in all cities and medium-sized towns. Most allow you to withdraw either dollars or colones, though local fees may apply. Credit and debit cards are widely used, but it's smart to carry cash when heading into rural areas or small beach towns. Tipping is not mandatory but is appreciated — around **10% in restaurants** and small tips for guides, porters, and drivers go a long way.

In terms of entry, travelers from the **U.S., Canada, EU, UK, Australia**, and many other countries are granted a **90-day tourist visa on arrival**. This comes with a catch: you must have a **proof of onward travel** — usually a return flight or a bus ticket leaving Costa Rica — or risk being denied boarding at your point of departure.

No vaccines are required for entry, except if you're arriving from a country with risk of yellow fever (like parts of South America or Sub-Saharan Africa), in which case proof of vaccination is mandatory.

However, doctors recommend being up to date on **hepatitis A, typhoid, and tetanus**, especially if you plan to explore jungles, eat street food, or visit small rural communities. Mosquito-borne diseases are present — including **dengue, chikungunya**, and **Zika** — so prevention is key: wear long sleeves, use DEET-based repellents, and choose accommodations with screens or nets in lower-elevation areas.

Chapter 2: When to Go & Where to Start

"In Costa Rica, we don't have four seasons. We have two: the green season... and paradise." – Local Saying

Costa Rica isn't a destination you simply visit — it's one you experience with your senses fully turned on. But timing, as in all great stories, can make the difference between a good trip and an unforgettable one. Whether you're craving sun-drenched beaches, mist-covered volcanoes, or wildlife encounters straight out of National Geographic, **when** you go — and **how** you begin — can completely shape your journey.

Most first-time travelers are surprised to learn that Costa Rica's weather doesn't follow the typical spring-summer-fall pattern. Instead, it operates on a rhythm of **wet and dry seasons** that vary by region. And that's where the magic — and the complexity — begins.

2.1 Best Times to Visit (Month-by-Month Breakdown)

Costa Rica's climate is tropical, but thanks to its topography, **you can experience jungle humidity, mountain chill, and dry heat — all in the same day**. Generally, the **dry season ("verano") runs from December to April**, and the **wet season ("invierno") stretches from May to November**. But don't be fooled by the terms. Rainy season doesn't mean constant downpour. It often brings short, intense showers in the afternoon with sunny mornings — and fewer tourists.

Here's what to expect month by month:

January & February

The peak of the dry season, and one of the most popular times to visit. Beaches are golden, skies are blue, and adventure outfitters are running at full steam. Wildlife is abundant, particularly in areas like Manuel Antonio and the Osa Peninsula. But expect higher prices and crowds, especially around New Year and Semana Santa (Holy Week). Make reservations early — the country buzzes with international visitors and locals alike.

March & April

Still in the dry season, these months bring rising temperatures and, in some regions, the first hints of the rainy season by late April. Guanacaste becomes a favorite for spring travelers, and it's one of the best times for beach lounging. Inland areas like Arenal and Monteverde are clear and accessible, perfect for zip-lining or volcano hikes. If you're planning on Easter travel, be mindful — it's a major holiday here and some towns virtually shut down, while others are packed.

May

The "shoulder season" begins. Rains return in short, daily bursts, but prices drop and crowds thin. This is a **sweet spot** for travelers who want value without sacrificing the experience. The country begins to green dramatically — hence the affectionate nickname "green season." Surf is up on both coasts, and nature is at its vibrant best. Great time for photography and slow travel.

June & July

June begins with consistent rains in the afternoons, especially in mountainous areas. Yet, there's often a short, unexpected dry spell in July called the **"veranillo de San Juan"** — a mini summer that surprises travelers with blue skies and beach days. Wildlife lovers rejoice: sea turtle nesting begins on the Caribbean coast, and humpback whales start appearing off the Pacific shores.

August
A month of contrasts. While the Pacific gets drenched, the **Caribbean is unusually dry**, offering unique travel opportunities to normally wetter areas like Tortuguero. Roads in more remote areas can get muddy and occasionally impassable, so stick to well-connected towns unless you're looking for an off-road adventure. Budget-conscious travelers can stretch their money here, especially for eco-lodges and long-term stays.

September & October

These are **the wettest months** in most of the country. Some hotels close, and transport options can be limited. That said, savvy travelers know that this is the **perfect time for the Caribbean side** — Puerto Viejo, Cahuita, and the surrounding areas enjoy some of their sunniest weather of the year. Rainforest lodges are lush and almost surreal in beauty. Just don't plan to rely on dry socks — bring quick-dry everything.

November
Transition month. Rains begin to ease, especially by mid-November. The landscapes are radiant, rivers are full for rafting, and the crowds haven't yet arrived. Surf is strong, prices are moderate, and wildlife is active. This is an

excellent month to begin your trip if you're aiming to avoid peak-season chaos but still enjoy good weather.

December
The dry season returns. Early December is ideal: weather is beautiful, but the holiday rush hasn't peaked. By the third week, tourism spikes again — flights and accommodations fill fast. But for many, the festive vibe, Christmas parades, fireworks, and beach parties are all part of Costa Rica's appeal. It's warm, sunny, and full of energy — a spectacular way to end the year.

The beauty of Costa Rica is that there's **no wrong time to visit**, only **different versions of the experience**. If you want perfect weather and don't mind the crowds, aim for December through April. If you're more interested in authenticity, value, and emerald-green landscapes, the "green season" months are your ticket. Either way, knowing **where to begin** your journey can help set the tone for the rest of your adventure.

2.2 Custom Itineraries

No two travelers come to Costa Rica for the same reason. Some want to surf at sunrise and sip cocktails by sunset. Others seek out toucans, thermal springs, or jungle hiking trails with no one in sight. That's why we've designed these customizable itineraries to match a range of travel styles, timeframes, and goals.

2.2.1 7 Days in Costa Rica (Highlights Only)

A week may not be enough to see it all — but it's enough to **fall in love with Costa Rica**. Start in **San José**, not because it's the most beautiful city, but because it gives you the lay of the land. Spend a day exploring the Central Market, the National Theatre, and getting your bearings.

Then head north to **La Fortuna**, home of the Arenal Volcano. It's the perfect mix of scenery and activity. Zip-lining, waterfall hikes, and hot springs fill your itinerary quickly. Don't rush — a slow soak at Tabacón or EcoTermales is more rewarding than ticking off a list.

From here, journey west to the beaches of **Tamarindo** or **Manuel Antonio**. One gives you surf, sun, and a bit of nightlife; the other surrounds you with wildlife and national park trails just minutes from your hotel. Wrap your trip with a lazy beach day before heading back to the capital.

This itinerary is fast-paced, but it captures the essence: **volcanoes, jungle, beaches, wildlife, and Pura Vida** — all in seven days.

2.2.2 14-Day Explorer's Journey

If a week gives you a taste, two weeks allows you to truly absorb Costa Rica's incredible diversity. This itinerary is designed for the traveler who wants it all — cloud forests, coastline, wildlife, and warm, unforgettable human encounters — without racing through the experience.

Day 1–2: San José & Central Highlands

Start in San José, but don't linger too long. Use your first full day to adjust, stroll Avenida Central, maybe grab coffee at a local roastery, and get a crash course in Costa Rican culture at the Pre-Columbian Gold Museum. Then head to the lush highlands of **Cartago**, where cooler air, winding roads, and views of **Irazú Volcano** offer a refreshing start.

Day 3–5: La Fortuna & Arenal Region

Next stop: the iconic **Arenal Volcano**. Spend three days here for hiking, wildlife watching, and adrenaline. Visit **La Fortuna Waterfall**, walk the hanging bridges, and book a night tour to spot sloths and kinkajous in the wild. There are hot springs aplenty, and no shame in visiting more than one — each has its own personality.

Day 6–8: Monteverde Cloud Forest

From La Fortuna, take the scenic route (and sometimes bumpy road) toward **Monteverde**, a high-elevation paradise where the mist clings to the trees and the sounds of howler monkeys echo through the forest. This is one of the best places for birdwatching — especially for catching a glimpse of the elusive **Resplendent Quetzal**. Walk the cloud forest trails early in the morning, then test your nerves with a canopy zip-line that stretches for miles.

Day 9–12: Pacific Coast — Manuel Antonio or Dominical

Head to the **Central Pacific** next. You have options: for beach + wildlife, **Manuel Antonio** is ideal — you'll walk through a national park in the morning and be swimming or paddleboarding by afternoon. For a more off-grid vibe, head slightly south to **Dominical**, a surfer town that's less polished but full of charm. Either way, sunsets here are legendary.

Day 13–14: Back to San José (via Tarcoles or Sarchí)

On your way back to the capital, stop at **Tarcoles River** to see massive crocodiles lounging beneath the bridge. If you enjoy crafts or want authentic souvenirs, take a detour through **Sarchí**, a colorful artisan town known for its hand-painted oxcarts and woodwork. Return to San José for a final night — relax, indulge in one last Casado, and reflect on the journey you've taken.

Two weeks lets you breathe in Costa Rica's rhythm — not just witness it, but *feel* it.

2.2.3 Family Adventure Route

Traveling Costa Rica as a family isn't just possible — it's encouraged. Locals are famously warm and family-oriented, and kids are often treated with genuine affection. This itinerary focuses on fun, safe, and enriching experiences for children of all ages, without sacrificing depth for the adults.

Begin in **San José** or **Alajuela**, where you can visit the **INBioparque** (an interactive biodiversity park) or the **Children's Museum**, both ideal for younger kids. After one or two nights, head to **La Fortuna**, where even the simplest activities feel adventurous: a boat ride across Lake Arenal, soaking in hot springs, horseback riding to the volcano. Parents will appreciate the excellent infrastructure, while kids will marvel at monkeys swinging overhead.

Continue to **Monteverde**, but pace yourself — this cloud forest region is cooler and calmer. Many eco-lodges offer child-friendly night walks, butterfly gardens, or frog exhibits. Even zip-lining is possible for children over a certain age (usually 6 or 7, depending on the company).

For your beach days, choose **Playa Samara** or **Tamarindo**. These beaches have calm waters, gentle surf, and kid-friendly resorts. Try turtle-watching at **Ostional** if visiting in season. End the trip back in the Central Valley for a cultural wrap-up: try a chocolate-making workshop or cooking class that the whole family can enjoy.

Costa Rica offers more than entertainment — it gives families shared *experiences* that become lasting stories.

2.2.4 Romantic Getaway Itinerary

For couples seeking seclusion, adventure, and intimacy, Costa Rica delivers on all fronts. It's not about luxury in the traditional sense — though five-star eco-lodges certainly exist — but more about **privacy, natural beauty, and unforgettable settings**.

Start in **Arenal**. Book a room with volcano views and an open-air hot tub. Most boutique hotels in this area offer candlelit dinners, spa services, and private tours — think sunset kayaking, couple's mud baths, or waterfall picnics.

From there, head south to **Montezuma** or **Santa Teresa** on the Nicoya Peninsula. These are bohemian coastal towns that blend jungle and beach with yoga retreats, fusion cuisine, and horses trotting along the shoreline at dusk. Wake up with the waves, explore tide pools in the afternoon, and dine barefoot in the sand by night.

Include a stay in **Osa Peninsula** if time and budget allow. It's harder to get to, but more remote and raw than anywhere else. Some lodges in **Drake Bay** or **Corcovado** can only be reached by boat, making the experience feel like your own tropical hideaway.

This itinerary is about slowing down, reconnecting, and letting the world fall away — one sunset, one hammock, one rainforest kiss at a time.

2.2.5 Backpacker's Budget Trail

Costa Rica has a reputation for being pricier than its Central American neighbors, but that doesn't mean it's off-limits for budget travelers. In fact, with careful planning, it can be one of the most **authentic and affordable travel experiences** you'll ever have.

Start in **Alajuela** — it's closer to the airport than San José and has several hostels with great reviews. Catch an early bus to **La Fortuna**, where you can hike to the waterfall on your own (just a small entrance fee), enjoy free hot springs like **Los Laureles**, and eat at family-run sodas.

Next, move to **Monteverde**, where you'll find $10 dorm beds, and community-run night hikes that cost half what the tour operators charge. Don't skip out on the adventure — you can do a canopy tour for less than $50 if you book in person rather than online.

Head west to **Santa Teresa** or **Puerto Viejo**, depending on your preferred coast. These towns are built for backpackers — surfboard rentals, beach hammocks, group yoga, cheap eats. You'll meet people from all over the world, share rides, swap hostel recommendations, and maybe even change your plans entirely — as many travelers do when they realize Costa Rica doesn't let go easily.

Public buses are frequent and incredibly cheap. Stick to local sodas for meals. Skip guided tours unless necessary. And always ask locals — they'll tell you where the real treasures are, and they'll usually point you there with a smile.

2.3 Packing Smart for the Tropics

Packing for Costa Rica isn't just about what to bring — it's about **what to leave behind**, too. Forget high heels, heavy sweaters, or "emergency" gear that just adds weight. What you need is flexibility, breathability, and a readiness to face sun, sweat, rain, and possibly mud — all in a single afternoon.

Start with the basics: lightweight, quick-dry clothing. Long sleeves are useful not for warmth, but for **mosquito protection and sun exposure**. Invest in a good **rain jacket**, not a disposable poncho — the storms here are real, especially in the green season. Footwear should be limited to **sturdy hiking shoes or trail runners**, and **comfortable sandals**. You'll rarely need more.

Don't forget a **daypack** that can double as your carry-on — it should be water-resistant and big enough to hold your camera, snacks, and travel documents. Speaking of documents, make photocopies of your passport and store them separately. Internet is widely available, but don't rely on cloud storage alone.

Bring **reef-safe sunscreen** — not only for your skin, but for the health of Costa Rica's delicate marine ecosystems. And if you're headed to rural or jungle areas, **a headlamp or small flashlight** is worth its weight in gold when the power flickers (which it sometimes does).

The most common mistake travelers make is **overpacking**. You'll likely wear the same few items repeatedly, especially if you're moving between regions. And if you forget something? Don't worry — Costa Rica's towns and cities have everything you need, often with a friendly local ready to help you find it.

Chapter 3: Getting In & Around

"Airports are only the beginning of an adventure. It's what lies beyond the terminal that defines the journey." — **Anonymous traveler in San José**

3.1 Airports & Entry Points

For most visitors to Costa Rica, the first breath of humid tropical air comes as they exit the aircraft at **Juan Santamaría International Airport (SJO)** in **Alajuela**, just outside **San José**. Handling the bulk of international arrivals, SJO is the country's busiest airport, known for its efficient customs process, clear signage in both English and Spanish, and proximity to the capital's hotels, restaurants, and transportation hubs.

On the opposite coast, **Daniel Oduber Quirós International Airport (LIR)** in **Liberia** has become the go-to entry point for travelers heading straight to the Pacific beaches of Guanacaste, Papagayo Peninsula, or the Nicoya Peninsula. In recent years, Liberia has undergone expansions to accommodate rising tourism from North America and Europe. For those flying in from the U.S., Canada, or Latin America, direct flights to both airports are increasingly common, especially during the high season between December and April.

There are also several **regional airports** that handle domestic flights or occasional chartered planes. These include **Tobías Bolaños Airport** in Pavas (San José), which primarily handles domestic travel, and smaller runways scattered throughout beach towns like Quepos (for Manuel Antonio) and Tambor (Nicoya Peninsula). Domestic airlines such as **Sansa Airlines** and **Green Airways** operate small planes that can be booked in advance or sometimes at the last minute — though schedules may shift due to weather or low demand.

Travelers entering overland from **Nicaragua** (through Peñas Blancas) or **Panama** (via Paso Canoas or Sixaola) should expect a slower process. These crossings are legal and commonly used, but often require more patience, as border infrastructure is limited and lines can be long during peak periods. Regardless of your entry point, immigration officials will ask for proof of onward travel and occasionally require travel insurance — a lingering policy from the pandemic era.

Travelers should confirm **visa requirements** before departure, though most Western passport holders (including the U.S., Canada, EU, and U.K.) are allowed to enter **visa-free for 90 days**. That said, Costa Rica is strict about overstays and increasingly checks departure proof at the time of entry.

3.2 Local Transport: Planes, Buses, Shuttles, Boats

Once inside Costa Rica, the real challenge — and thrill — becomes how to get from point A to point B. The country offers a surprisingly diverse array of transport options, ranging from air taxis to riverboats, though each mode has its quirks.

For budget travelers and cultural purists, **the public bus system** is not only affordable, but also reliable in most areas. Long-distance buses like **Tica Bus**, **TransNica**, and **Tracopa** connect major cities and towns with fares that rarely exceed a few dollars. These buses depart from terminals that can feel chaotic to first-time visitors but are usually safe and manageable with basic Spanish. Do note: exact change is often required for city buses, and signage can be minimal in rural zones.

Shared shuttles are an increasingly popular mid-range option. Services such as **Interbus**, **Gray Line**, and **Easy Ride** offer air-conditioned vans that pick travelers up from hotels and drop them directly at their next destination. They're more expensive than public buses but far more comfortable and faster. Book in advance, especially during high season or holiday weeks.

Domestic flights are a time-saving luxury if you're traveling from San José to more remote areas such as the Osa Peninsula or Tortuguero. These short hops can turn a 7-hour road journey into a 45-minute scenic flight — though luggage restrictions are strict, and cancellations due to weather are not uncommon.

Then there's the **boat travel** — essential in areas like **Tortuguero** and parts of the **Nicoya Peninsula**. Water taxis shuttle guests between mainland terminals and island-like regions cut off by rivers, swamps, or ocean. The ride to Tortuguero, for example, winds through jungle canals and is arguably part of the experience. Expect limited timetables and pack waterproof bags.

3.3 Renting a Car in Costa Rica: Tips & Warnings

Driving in Costa Rica offers a level of freedom that public transportation can't match. With your own set of wheels, secluded beaches, hot springs, and cloud forest trails suddenly become accessible on your schedule. But before picking up the keys, travelers should understand a few hard truths about the local driving culture.

First, **you must rent a 4x4** if you plan to explore beyond the Central Valley or Pacific coast. Many rural roads, particularly in Nicoya or around Arenal and Monteverde, are unpaved, riddled with potholes, and susceptible to washouts after heavy rains. Even some "highways" are better described as gravel tracks. A 4WD vehicle isn't just recommended — it's essential.

Second, Costa Rica has **mandatory insurance** that can dramatically raise the total rental cost. While your credit card or travel insurance may cover collision or theft, the government requires you to purchase third-party liability insurance from the rental agency — and this fee is non-negotiable. The base price you see online is rarely the price you pay.

Driving habits vary. In urban areas like San José, expect sudden lane changes, minimal use of turn signals, and motorcycles weaving between cars at close range. In rural areas, roads are often narrow with poor lighting, and local drivers may stop without warning to greet neighbors or let livestock cross.

GPS apps like **Waze** are far more accurate than Google Maps in Costa Rica and are widely used by locals. That said, signal coverage is patchy in remote zones. Download offline maps ahead of time and consider purchasing a local SIM card for better navigation and emergency connectivity.

Parking is another consideration. Street parking in cities is often chaotic, and cars can be towed or fined without clear signage. Many hotels offer private lots, and some beaches now have local attendants offering paid "watchman" services for parked vehicles — always tip them.

3.4 Road Conditions, GPS Apps & Signage

One of the most misunderstood aspects of travel in Costa Rica is the condition of its road network. While the government has made strides in infrastructure over the last decade, the country's mountainous terrain, seasonal rainfall, and limited maintenance budgets mean that **road quality is inconsistent at best**.

Major highways, such as **Route 27** (San José to the Pacific coast) and **Route 1** (the Inter-American Highway), are paved and generally well maintained. However, these roads often narrow to a single lane in each direction and can become clogged with trucks and slow traffic, especially on weekends and holidays.

The further you go from major towns, the more unpredictable the roads become. Expect potholes, washed-out shoulders, and even stretches of road that vanish into dirt paths. Bridges in remote areas can be one-lane, unlit, or made of planks that shift beneath your tires. Speed bumps — known locally as *muertos* (literally "dead men") — appear without warning and are often unmarked.

Signage is a mixed bag. In major tourist regions, you'll find English-translated signs pointing toward landmarks and popular towns. In others, signage may be absent, confusing, or graffiti-covered. Addresses are rarely used in the traditional sense. Instead, directions are given based on landmarks ("200 meters east of the church" is a common one). Understanding this cultural norm is essential when driving or asking for help.

As mentioned earlier, **Waze** reigns supreme in Costa Rica. It offers crowd-sourced updates on traffic, police checkpoints, road closures, and hazards. **Google Maps**, though improving, can lead drivers into unpaved or blocked routes. If you're traveling to areas known for poor roads, consider calling your hotel or guide in advance to confirm accessibility — especially during the rainy season.

What's remarkable is how many travelers, even those who arrive wary, leave Costa Rica saying the road trips were among their favorite memories. The unpredictability becomes part of the story. A wrong turn might lead to a secluded waterfall. A delayed drive could result in seeing toucans fly overhead. In Costa Rica, transportation isn't just a means to an end — it's part of the adventure.

Part 2: Destination Deep Dive – Region by Region

Chapter 4: San José & Central Valley

"San José is not the soul of Costa Rica, but it is the heartbeat — the rhythm you can't ignore, even if you're just passing through." — **Anonymous Costa Rican taxi driver**

At first glance, San José may seem like the kind of capital city travelers rush through on their way to the beaches, jungles, or volcanoes. It's noisy. It's unpredictable. It's not trying to be pretty. And yet, for those who spend more than a night here, the city begins to reveal its layers — not in grand gestures, but in vibrant street corners, surprising colonial facades, and the soft echoes of marimba music floating from an open courtyard.

The Central Valley — home to nearly two-thirds of the Costa Rican population — cradles this buzzing metropolis with its highland breezes and fertile hillsides. It's a region of contrast and culture: a place where you can sip world-class coffee at sunrise and stroll through a gold museum before noon. It's also your best access point to some of Costa Rica's most iconic natural wonders, all within a short drive.

Whether you're here for a few hours or a few days, this chapter will help you see San José and its surrounding valley for what they truly are: not just a gateway, but a destination in their own right.

4.1 Must-See: National Theatre, Gold & Jade Museums

Teatro Nacional

Walking down Avenida Segunda, the city's main artery, you could almost miss it if you're distracted — the grandeur of the **Teatro Nacional** doesn't shout. But step inside, and you'll feel the pride of a nation in marble and gilded balconies. Completed in 1897, the theatre was born of the coffee boom and financed by a tax the elite happily levied upon themselves. It remains one of Latin America's most beautiful performance venues, with French-style chandeliers, Italian frescoes, and Austrian ironwork — a baroque jewel box of European artistry in the heart of the tropics.

Even if you're not in town for an evening performance (which is highly recommended), the guided daytime tours are worth every colón. Docents lead you through stories of Costa Rica's golden age, pointing out details that speak volumes about the country's aspiration toward sophistication — and its deep love for the arts.

Pre-Columbian Gold Museum

Just a short walk away, the **Pre-Columbian Gold Museum** offers a radically different kind of beauty: the kind forged by indigenous hands centuries before Columbus arrived. Housed beneath the Plaza de la Cultura in a space that feels part bunker, part shrine, the museum displays over 1,600 artifacts of shimmering craftsmanship — animal figurines, ceremonial discs, and delicate jewelry — all telling the story of Costa Rica's original inhabitants and their relationship to nature, power, and the divine.

Jade Museum

Equally compelling is the **Jade Museum**, which sits in a sleek modern building just a few blocks east. Less frequented but increasingly praised, this museum holds the largest collection of American jade in the world. The exhibit design is immersive: dimly lit corridors mimic rainforest pathways, and interactive displays bring the ancient world to life. It's not just about the stones — it's about storytelling. About time. About identity.

Together, these three sites form a cultural triangle that's entirely walkable and immensely rewarding. For many visitors, it's here — in San José's unexpectedly rich museum scene — that Costa Rica's history comes into clearer focus.

4.2 Nightlife, Cafés & Urban Culture

San José transforms after dark. While it's not a city known for an all-night party culture, it does offer a spectrum of nightlife that reflects its cosmopolitan leanings and youthful energy. You won't find mega-clubs, but you'll find craft beer dens, rooftop lounges, poetry slams, jazz bars, and speakeasy-style cocktail spots tucked behind unmarked doors.

Barrio Escalante, once a quiet residential zone, is now the epicenter of cool. This is where San José's culinary and creative class converge. Think twinkling fairy lights strung across open-air courtyards, microbreweries like Wilk or Costa Rica Beer Factory serving up IPAs with passionfruit notes, and gastropubs plating fusion dishes that reimagine gallo pinto with gourmet flair.

Café Miel

Just a few blocks away, **Barrio Amón** whispers of another era. Its old mansions, some now restored into bohemian cafés and small art galleries, feel almost European in charm. Grab a seat at **Café Miel** or **La Mancha**, order a cortado or a glass of local wine, and soak in the intellectual air. On weekends, you might stumble upon a street art festival, a tango pop-up, or an indie short film screening inside a converted garage.

Street culture is alive here too. Skaters roll through parks. Public murals pulse with political commentary. And everywhere — especially near the **National Park** and the university zones — you'll find music: reggae, rock en español, Latin jazz. It's not curated. It's not always polished. But it's real — and it's unmistakably San José.

4.3 Where to Stay: From Boutique to Budget

Accommodation in San José has come a long way in the past decade. What was once a city full of generic business hotels is now a hub for boutique hideaways, eco-luxury stays, and well-priced hostels with actual character.

Hotel Grano de Oro

For those looking to experience San José with style, **Hotel Grano de Oro** on Paseo Colón is a timeless pick. Housed in a converted Victorian mansion, it offers old-world elegance — four-poster beds, stained-glass windows, lush courtyards — with modern amenities and a restaurant that's among the city's best. Prices here hover around $170–$220 per night, depending on the season, but it's worth every dollar for travelers seeking comfort and history.

Urban Green Hotel & Suites

In **Barrio Escalante**, you'll find a wave of design-forward accommodations like **Eco Stay Costa Rica** and **Urban Green Hotel & Suites**, where nightly rates range from $80 to $120. These hotels tend to focus on sustainability, with reclaimed wood furniture, solar power, and breakfasts made from locally sourced produce. They're ideal for digital nomads, couples, and urban explorers who want a blend of aesthetics and ethics.

For budget-conscious travelers, there are excellent options too. **Selina San José** blends a hostel vibe with co-working spaces, wellness events, and modern dorms or private rooms.

Prices start around $25 for a shared room and $65 for private ones. It's social, convenient, and positioned in a neighborhood that feels secure for solo travelers.

Selina San José

Hotel La Rosa de América,

And if you're just passing through for a night or two before heading out to La Fortuna or Manuel Antonio, the airport-adjacent town of **Alajuela** (technically outside San José but close enough to count) offers clean and affordable guesthouses like **Hotel La Rosa de América**, where you can sleep peacefully for under $90 and still be only 15 minutes from the terminal.

More than just a place to sleep, where you stay in San José can shape your experience of the city. Choose a place that invites you to linger, not just rest.

4.4 Day Trips: Poás Volcano, Coffee Farms & Waterfalls

For all its urban appeal, San José's greatest gift might be how easily you can escape it. Within just an hour or two of the capital, the Central Valley opens into a landscape stitched with volcanoes, misty cloud forests, terraced coffee farms, and cascading waterfalls. Day trips here don't feel rushed — they feel like a complete change of pace. You'll leave the concrete behind, and by the time you take your first breath of high-altitude air, you'll wonder how such wilderness coexists so close to the country's busiest city.

Poás Volcano National Park

The crown jewel of day trips from San José is **Poás Volcano National Park**. Located about 50 km northwest of the city, it's one of the most accessible active volcanoes in the world — and one of the most dramatic. The main crater is nearly a mile wide and often steams like a giant kettle, surrounded by eerie lunar rock and sulfuric mist. The park has a strict entrance policy: timed reservations, limited capacity, and clear weather conditions. But if you get the timing right, the view is unforgettable — an immense, boiling, otherworldly bowl set inside dense cloud forest.

La Paz Waterfall Gardens

The drive to Poás is an experience in itself. It snakes through villages lined with fruit stands selling fresh strawberries and cheese empanadas. As you ascend, the air cools, the flora thickens, and suddenly you're above the clouds. Make a stop at **La Paz Waterfall Gardens**, a private nature park en route that offers close encounters with toucans, butterflies, and jaguars — yes, jaguars — in its animal sanctuary. But the real highlight is its five waterfalls, each one increasingly dramatic as you descend the forest trail. While it's more polished and curated than a true jungle hike, the experience is deeply immersive, especially for families or photographers chasing beauty with a tripod in hand.

Equally compelling — and arguably more essential to understanding Costa Rica — are the **coffee plantations** that blanket the highlands outside the city. Coffee isn't just a crop here; it's a cornerstone of national identity. In the late 1800s, it financed the National Theatre and shaped Costa Rica's early democracy. Today, it's a sustainable, high-quality export and a point of pride for producers and baristas alike.

Doka Estate

You'll find several excellent coffee tours within reach of San José. **Doka Estate**, near Alajuela, is one of the most popular. A family-owned operation, Doka walks visitors through the entire production process, from seedling to steaming cup. The tour includes a stroll through verdant coffee fields, a visit to the old-style wet mill (declared a historical and architectural heritage site), and of course, generous tastings. It's not just about the drink — it's a sensory and cultural deep dive.

Café Britt

If you're looking for something a little more intimate and off-the-beaten path, **Café Britt** in Heredia offers a theatrical, slightly cheeky spin on the traditional coffee tour — complete with comedic performances by multilingual guides who somehow make soil science and roasting profiles wildly entertaining.

Catarata del Toro

For travelers seeking natural beauty over caffeine buzz, there are dozens of **waterfalls** around the Central Valley that deserve a visit. **Catarata del Toro**, for instance, is a jaw-dropper — a 270-foot torrent plunging into the crater of an extinct volcano, surrounded by primary forest. It's less trafficked than La Paz and rewards those willing to tackle the steep stairs leading to its base. The drive from San José takes around 1.5 hours, but you'll pass through rustic mountain villages and cloud-wrapped scenery that make the journey as memorable as the destination.

Los Chorros Waterfalls

Another favorite is **Los Chorros Waterfalls** in Grecia — a short, relatively easy hike leads you to twin falls where locals often swim, picnic, and spend the day. It's raw, refreshing, and best of all, largely unspoiled by commercial tourism.

If you're staying longer in San José, consider stitching these day trips together into a two- or three-day circuit. Start with Poás in the morning, stop at a coffee farm on the way down, and overnight in a cozy lodge near the waterfalls. Or build an itinerary that starts in the city and ends in the mountains

— a reversal of the usual pattern, but one that feels more rooted, more immersive.

The beauty of basing yourself in San José isn't just convenience — it's the flexibility to experience the country's natural and cultural extremes without packing up and moving every night. With a good pair of walking shoes, an early start, and a bit of curiosity, the Central Valley becomes a treasure trove of daylong adventures that many travelers miss entirely. But you won't.

Chapter 5: Alajuela & Around

"There's something about this province… the air smells like coffee, the soil breathes smoke, and the road always leads to something unexpected." – A local guide in Fraijanes.

Alajuela isn't a detour from Costa Rica's main attractions — it *is* one. Often overshadowed by the buzz of San José or the beaches of Guanacaste, this highland province is where Costa Rica reveals its essence. The moment your tires roll past the outskirts of the capital, the urban haze lifts. Lush ridges cradle colonial towns, the landscape opens to sweeping coffee fields, and in the distance, Poás Volcano rests like a sleeping giant, its summit wreathed in cloud.

This region isn't just scenic — it's sensory. You hear the rustle of palm-sized leaves underfoot. You smell the morning steam rising from volcanic vents. You taste smoky, mineral-rich coffee before the beans ever touch milk or sugar. Alajuela holds the pulse of the country's natural rhythms — slower, deeper, and undeniably real.

5.1 Gateway to Adventure: La Paz Gardens & Poás Volcano

Less than 90 minutes from San José, the **La Paz Waterfall Gardens** aren't just a photo stop — they're a revelation. Five towering waterfalls carve their way through dense cloud forest, the tallest plunging over 120 feet into a gorge that echoes with the sound of pure force. But it's not just about the falls. The trails themselves — misty, stone-lined, slippery in the right way — thread through some of the richest biodiversity on Earth.

You'll pass hummingbird feeders alive with color and motion, an aviary that rehabilitates injured toucans and macaws, and the butterfly observatory where hundreds of wings brush silently against your shirt. There's a frog habitat where you'll learn to listen, not look, and a serpentarium that reminds you why hiking boots matter. Yes, it's curated — but it doesn't feel staged. It's wild enough to thrill and safe enough for families, photographers, and solo wanderers alike.

Continue north, and the **Poás Volcano National Park** awaits — home to one of the **largest active craters in the world**, stretching over a mile wide. On clear mornings (and there are few guarantees), the view into the crater is surreal: a turquoise acidic lake that belches sulfuric steam and ripples in constant motion. It looks alien. Unstable. Alive.

The air thins as you climb — over 2,700 meters above sea level — and the smell is unmistakable: sulfur, pine, and the faint sweetness of cold mountain air. The park authorities limit access in timed windows, both for safety and to preserve the fragile crater rim. Arrive early. Check weather conditions the night before. And bring layers; it's easy to forget you're in the tropics when temperatures here dip below 10°C.

Hike the **Sendero Botos trail** while you're there — a short loop that winds through dwarf forest and leads to the now-extinct Botos crater, filled with an emerald lake. It's less dramatic, more meditative. Fewer people take this trail, which is why you should.

5.2 Coffee Routes & Plantation Tours

Ask a Costa Rican what fuels their country, and coffee will be near the top of the list. Not just as a beverage — as a way of life. In **Alajuela's Central Highlands**, coffee isn't consumed; it's cultivated with pride, tradition, and a quiet reverence that's passed from generation to generation.

This is where **coffee tourism** actually feels personal. Drive through the hills of **Naranjo**, **San Ramón**, or **Grecia**, and the rows of coffee bushes stretch across volcanic slopes like stitched green tapestries — uniform, precise, thriving. The soil here is black and alive. The altitude is ideal. The flavor? Complex, citrusy, slightly nutty — influenced by elevation and minerals left behind by eruptions long past.

Visit **Doka Estate**, one of the most renowned plantations in the region, where the coffee process is still partially done with equipment that dates back over a century. A guide will walk you through the growing stages, from cherry to bean to cup, including the peeling, drying, roasting, and grading. But beyond the technicalities, they'll talk about *café culture* — how locals take their coffee slowly, mid-morning, often with a piece of sweet bread and no rush in sight.

Hacienda Alsacia

More boutique experiences await at **Hacienda Alsacia**, Starbucks' only working farm, which doubles as a research lab and showroom of sustainability. While it may feel like a corporate contrast to the mom-and-pop farms nearby, it also offers innovation, world-class barista training, and an incredible view of the valley below.

Prefer something smaller, quieter, less polished? Drive up to **Finca Rosa Blanca**, where organic farming blends seamlessly with eco-luxury. Or stop in at roadside stands along **Ruta 126**, where families sell sun-dried beans in reused jars, and will offer you a cup brewed in a chorreador if you smile and ask.

The best time to tour is between **November and March**, during the harvest. You'll see pickers (often Nicaraguan migrant workers) with red-stained hands moving through the bushes with woven baskets, working fast before the morning mist dries off the leaves. It's hard work. It's part of the story. And it's worth understanding.

5.3 Local Eats & Traditional Dishes

Alajuela isn't fancy when it comes to food — and that's a compliment. The city itself, the second largest in the country, thrives on **humble sodas**, open-air markets, and dishes that feed the body with simplicity and care.

gallo pinto

Start with **gallo pinto** in the morning — a blend of rice and beans infused with cilantro, peppers, onions, and Salsa Lizano (a sauce every traveler should try). Most sodas serve it alongside **huevos al gusto**, fried plantains, and local cheese. Add a hot tortilla and a cup of café negro, and you've eaten like 80% of Costa Ricans do each morning.

Lunch is often **casado**, which translates to "married" — a marriage of protein, rice, beans, salad, and fried banana. Pork chop? Fish filet? Grilled chicken? All options are common, and all pair beautifully with fresh guanábana juice or agua de tamarindo.

casado

Olla de Carne

Try **Olla de Carne** if you spot it on a menu. This slow-cooked beef and vegetable stew isn't available everywhere — it takes hours to prepare — but it captures the highland soul in a bowl: soft chunks of yuca, corn, green plantain, and meat that falls apart at the touch of a spoon.

Mercado Central

One hidden gem in central Alajuela is **Mercado Central**, a maze of stalls selling everything from herbs to spices to fried snacks. You can pick up empanadas hot from the fryer, or try a bowl of **sopa negra**, a black bean soup topped with a hardboiled egg and packed with flavor that's both earthy and clean.

In the outskirts, especially near coffee towns, watch for wood-fire rotisserie chicken spots and roadside **panaderías** — bakeries — where locals line up for fresh **pan dulce** before the afternoon rain hits.

This is food made with purpose. Not for trends or presentation, but for nourishment, pride, and flavor that doesn't need translating.

5.4 Practical Travel Tips for Exploring Alajuela

Alajuela may be only a short distance from San José, but travel here runs on a very different rhythm. The pace is slower, less frenetic, and more in tune with the natural world. While the proximity to the capital makes it a convenient jumping-off point, the region demands a bit of local knowledge to truly appreciate what it offers — and to avoid common pitfalls that travelers often encounter.

First, let's talk about **transportation**. If you plan on seeing more than just the city center or the major tourist stops like La Paz and Poás, **renting a car is essential**. Public transport is available — buses run from San José to Alajuela regularly, and there are local colectivos within town — but for anyone wanting to explore the countryside, visit coffee farms, or stay in rural lodges, relying on buses quickly becomes limiting. Roads can be narrow and steep in areas like Fraijanes or San Isidro, but they're paved and safe to drive, as long as you don't rush. Waze is the most reliable navigation app used locally.

Gas stations are frequent along main routes, but be aware: **most are full-service**, and attendants expect small tips for fueling or windshield cleaning. Carry cash — especially small denominations of colones. Many rural shops and cafés still operate without card readers or change for large bills.

Speaking of cash, **prices in Alajuela are lower than in coastal tourist areas**, and street food or market snacks can cost under $3 USD. That said, don't expect everything to be "cheap." Tours, park entry fees, and accommodations — particularly eco-lodges or coffee estates — may still reflect the country's national pricing strategy for tourists. It's not about gouging; it's about sustaining fragile economies and supporting local business models that aim for quality over quantity.

As for **lodging**, Alajuela city has an increasing number of boutique hotels and stylish B&Bs that cater to travelers using the nearby airport (SJO) — but these often lack character. If you want a more authentic stay, look outside the city center: **Grecia** and **Sarchí** offer peaceful mountain accommodations, often family-run, where you wake to birdsong instead of traffic. **Eco-lodges** near Poás and Vara Blanca offer forest immersion and often include private guides or farm-to-table meals. It's not uncommon to find lodges with cloud forest views that cost half what they would in Monteverde, without sacrificing comfort or service.

While Alajuela is largely safe — especially during the day — **keep your belongings secure in crowded public markets or transport terminals**. Petty theft isn't rampant, but like any growing urban area, it exists. Avoid flashing expensive electronics or leaving bags unattended, particularly in busier parts of the central district.

One of the unexpected highlights in this region is the people. Ticos in Alajuela are known for their **warmth and casual humor**, often making jokes with strangers or offering unsolicited directions if they see you looking confused. A little Spanish goes a long way. If you can manage even a basic "Buenos días" or "¿Dónde está...?", you'll often be rewarded with a smile, or even better — a shortcut you didn't know existed.

Finally, a word about the **weather**. The climate in Alajuela is distinctly milder than the coasts — especially in higher elevation towns like San Pedro de Poás or Zarcero. Days are warm and dry in the dry season (December to April), while afternoons during the green season (May to November) bring heavy, cooling rains. Don't trust blue skies in the morning — always bring a light waterproof layer, especially if you're hiking or venturing beyond the urban areas.

Sunsets here, especially from the hills above the city, are spectacular — fiery orange skies that turn the coffee fields gold before dipping behind mountain silhouettes. It's the kind of light photographers chase and the kind of moment travelers remember long after they've gone.

Chapter 6: Cartago & Orosi Valley

"Faith and nature are the twin architects of Cartago's soul. One carved sanctuaries of stone, the other sculpted valleys of steam and silence."

Less than an hour southeast of San José, the province of **Cartago** unfolds like a quiet secret — serene, spiritual, and steeped in history. Unlike the boisterous beaches of Guanacaste or the tourist-trodden trails of Manuel Antonio, Cartago doesn't compete for attention. It doesn't need to. It offers something far more enduring: **authenticity, elevation, and ease**. From the reverent hush inside a centuries-old basilica to the otherworldly chill atop a stratovolcano, to the warm silence of geothermal pools deep in the Orosi Valley — this chapter is for the traveler who seeks both **stillness and spectacle**.

6.1 Spiritual and Scenic: Basilica de Los Ángeles

At the heart of Cartago lies a structure that transcends architecture. The **Basílica de Nuestra Señora de los Ángeles**, built in 1639 and rebuilt after multiple earthquakes, isn't just a church. It's a pilgrimage site. A spiritual anchor. A place where belief becomes movement — quite literally.

Basílica de Nuestra Señora de los Ángeles

Every August 2nd, over a **million Costa Ricans** make the journey to this basilica on foot, some from as far away as Guanacaste. Known as *La Romería*, this annual pilgrimage honors **La Negrita**, Costa Rica's patron saint — a small, black Madonna statue believed to have miraculous healing powers. Whether you're religious or not, the scale and sincerity of this event are deeply moving. If you visit around that date, expect blocked roads, packed plazas, and a reverence that vibrates in the air.

Outside of pilgrimage season, the basilica welcomes visitors daily. Step inside, and the first thing you'll notice is the **distinct Moorish-Byzantine design** — arches and windows that feel more like a sacred poem than stonework. Light filters through colored glass, painting the tiled floors with muted golds and blues. Along the back wall, the tiny statue of La Negrita rests in a golden casing. Below the basilica, a crypt and spring reputed for its healing properties continue to draw devotees who bottle the water in silence and prayer.

You don't need to attend mass to appreciate the space. Simply **sit on one of the benches** and observe — the locals who drop in for a quick prayer, the elderly lighting candles, the travelers marveling quietly. Just outside, vendors sell rosaries, religious art, and caramelized peanuts. Time here bends. It doesn't rush.

6.2 Irazú Volcano & Hidden Thermal Springs

From the spiritual to the surreal, drive just over 30 kilometers from Cartago's city center and the temperature begins to dip. The air thins. Suddenly, you're standing 3,432 meters above sea level, looking into a crater the color of mint ice cream.

Irazú Volcano, Costa Rica's tallest active volcano, offers a view like no other — on especially clear mornings, you can see both the **Pacific and Atlantic Oceans** from the summit. But don't let Instagram fool you: fog often drapes the crater without warning, giving the place a haunting beauty that's no less thrilling.

Irazú Volcano

The drive up is steep but smooth, passing dairy farms, mist-covered eucalyptus trees, and roadside stalls selling hot empanadas. Once inside the national park (entrance fee ~ $15 for foreigners), you'll find a **well-maintained path** to the main crater. There's no hiking required — it's accessible even to those with mobility limitations. The cold is biting, though, so bring a warm layer, especially early in the morning.

Orosi Valley

From Irazú, continue your descent southeast into the **Orosi Valley** — and enter a landscape of deep greens, thermal steam, and utter calm. Here, the mountains fold inward like quiet giants, and the Pacuare River winds its way through coffee farms and colonial churches. While the valley is known for its historic towns and fertile soil, it's the **hidden hot springs** that offer some of the most restorative experiences in the region.

Balneario de Aguas Termales Orosi.

One such place is **Balneario de Aguas Termales Orosi**. Tucked behind a local soccer field and open to the public, this is not a luxury spa — but a **charming, affordable** set of natural thermal pools. Entrance is just $4–6, and you'll be soaking with locals beneath dense canopies of bamboo and palm. The water smells faintly of minerals but is clean, warm, and deeply relaxing. You'll often hear toucans in the trees above and the laughter of children echoing from the adjacent play area.

Termales del Bosque

For something more upscale, try **Termales del Bosque**, located on the edge of the valley. It features **private forested soaking pools**, quiet walking trails, and optional spa treatments. Here, prices range from **$20 for a day pass** to **$85–$150 per night** for lodging with thermal access included.

6.3 Best Boutique Hotels & Wellness Escapes (With Cost Breakdown)

Cartago and Orosi are not hotel-heavy regions, but that's part of their charm. What you do find here are **handpicked gems** — locally run, beautifully designed, and steeped in tranquility.

Start with **Hotel Boutique La Casona del Cafetal**, perched above Lake Cachí. Surrounded by coffee plantations and bougainvillea blooms, this colonial-style retreat is perfect for couples and solo travelers seeking privacy and views. Rooms begin at **$95 per night**, including breakfast with locally sourced fruit, gallo pinto, and fresh-pressed juice. The on-site restaurant, set under a grand almond tree, is a favorite even among Cartago locals.

Hotel Boutique La Casona del Cafetal

Orosi Lodge

In downtown Orosi, **Orosi Lodge** offers something more minimalist but no less memorable. With German-Costa Rican ownership, the vibe is laid-back European meets rainforest chic. Rates hover around **$75–$90 per night**, and every room comes with panoramic views of the volcano and valley. There's also a small café on-site serving rich Orosi-grown coffee and homemade pastries.

Rio Perlas Spa & Resort

For travelers looking to pair accommodation with wellness, **Rio Perlas Spa & Resort** offers the full package. Located between Cartago and Orosi, this larger estate includes **thermal pools, a full spa, and horseback riding**. Rooms are around **$130–$180 per night**, and the setting — enveloped in foggy rainforest and birdsong — feels almost cinematic.

Lastly, for the deeply unplugged experience, consider **Rancho Naturalista**, a birdwatching haven further southeast. While slightly more remote, it's a sanctuary for eco-tourists and photographers. Rates start around **$150–$200 per night**, including full-board meals and guided nature walks.

Rancho Naturalista

Each of these stays reflects something essential about Cartago and Orosi: the rhythm is slower, the spaces quieter, and the sense of place — undeniable. Whether you're waking to the sound of a distant church bell or the hiss of steam rising from a valley spring, what you feel here isn't just peace. It's presence.

Chapter 7: Heredia

"In Heredia, the real Costa Rica whispers through the rhythm of everyday life — in the morning scent of roasted coffee, the laughter echoing from narrow streets, and the sizzle of something delicious just around the corner."

7.1 Cultural Hotspot Near the Capital

Heredia rarely makes the headlines in glossy travel magazines, and that's exactly its charm. Located just 10 kilometers from the capital city, San José, this unassuming province unfolds like a well-kept secret — intimate, authentic, and quietly confident. It doesn't demand attention with grand attractions or over-polished experiences. Instead, Heredia invites travelers to slow down and notice the details: the chipped tiles on an old colonial church, the hand-painted café signs, the locals calling each other "mae" over strong coffee at dawn.

Known as *La Ciudad de las Flores* — the City of Flowers — Heredia's nickname once referred to the abundance of blooming gardens. But today, the real "flowers" here are its people and culture. Much of the city's daily life is influenced by its universities, particularly the National University of Costa Rica, which infuses the area with youthful energy, political activism, art, and conversation. Walk down any given block in the city center and you might hear a student band rehearsing in the courtyard of a colonial building, or find a makeshift poetry reading at a tiny café.

Unlike the more polished, tourist-centric areas of the country, Heredia holds onto its Costa Rican soul. It's a city of local rhythms: of mothers carrying baskets through the market, of old men arguing about football in the park, of baristas who know your order before you say it. The streets are narrow, the sidewalks uneven, but they're filled with life. There's no curated experience here — just experience.

Iglesia de la Inmaculada

Architecturally, Heredia is a mix of time periods. Colonial-era buildings like the iconic *Iglesia de la Inmaculada* — completed in the late 18th century — still stand, anchoring the historical core. Side streets reveal simple houses with brightly painted walls, wrought iron window guards, and tiled roofs that seem to bake in the dry-season sun. And amid it all, a modern rhythm: cafes buzzing with laptop screens, scooters weaving between taxis, students laughing over late-night snacks.

Heredia is also the beginning of many unexpected journeys. A short drive away, coffee plantations stretch across the hillsides like living stories — each finca (farm) offering a glimpse into one of Costa Rica's most defining traditions. A bit farther up, the air cools and the views open into misty valleys, hinting at the adventure-rich northwestern highlands. But Heredia itself? It's where you come not to escape, but to *be*.

7.2 Traditional Markets, Food Tours & Artisan Stops

The **Mercado Central de Heredia** isn't flashy. You won't find sleek signage or English-speaking guides. What you'll find instead is authenticity by the handful. Step inside, and you're hit with the layered aroma of fresh cilantro, just-ground coffee, ripe bananas, fried plantains, and the earthy scent of tortillas heating on a metal comal. The stalls are small but overflowing — not just with products, but with stories.

A butcher sharpens his knife while chatting with a longtime customer about the local football team. A woman in an apron offers samples of homemade tamales, wrapped in banana leaves and tied with string. In the corner, a quiet vendor with a kind face sells handwoven baskets and pottery etched with pre-Columbian designs — work passed down through generations. You'll find produce so fresh the dew still clings to the lettuce, and cheeses molded into perfect wheels resting in coolers beside hand-labeled yogurt jars.

Outside the market, several **walking food tours** have cropped up in recent years, quietly building a reputation among those in the know. One tour takes you from an old soda (a small family-run diner) into a hidden bakery, through an artisanal chocolate studio, and ends at a rooftop bar overlooking the mountains — all the while weaving in local folklore and the evolution of Costa Rican cuisine.

Perhaps the most rewarding stops are the small **artisan workshops** tucked into residential neighborhoods. Some are no more than converted garages where artists craft by hand — woodworking, leather goods, recycled-material jewelry. They're not on TripAdvisor, but they are on WhatsApp, and a friendly local will likely guide you there if you ask. These artists often don't sell online. Their customers are neighbors and friends, and when you buy something, it's not just a souvenir — it's a part of Heredia's living culture.

Coffee, of course, deserves its own mention. Though better known as the gateway to the coffee-growing highlands, Heredia has its own micro-roasters. You can sit down in a narrow café, watch beans roasted in small batches, and taste brews that never make it to export. Try the *Chemex* brew at Café Privado, or a rich *chorreado* (traditional drip method) at a street cart. Locals often pair their coffee with a *pan de elote* (corn cake) or *empanada de chiverre* (sweet squash turnover), and they'll happily explain what makes it special — if you ask in Spanish, even better.

7.3 Best Eats on a Budget

If you know where to look, Heredia might just be the best place in Costa Rica to eat like a local — and do it affordably. While San José's food scene grows more international and touristy by the year, Heredia remains grounded in family-run *sodas*, budget-friendly bakeries, and unpretentious street food stalls where meals rarely break the $5 mark.

Start with **Soda El Kora**, tucked away on Calle 9 near UNA University. The decor is minimal — metal chairs, plastic tablecloths — but the food is unbeatable. Order a *casado con cerdo en salsa* (pork in savory sauce, served with rice, beans, plantains, and salad) and you'll understand why it's always packed at lunchtime. Locals from all walks of life gather here: professors, taxi drivers, students, street vendors. It's as democratic as food gets.

Another gem, especially for early risers, is **El Puesto del Sabor**, a late-night and early-morning favorite near Parque Central. Their *gallo pinto con huevo y natilla* — Costa Rica's signature breakfast of rice and beans with eggs and sour cream — tastes even better when eaten on a stool under flickering fluorescent lights, listening to an AM radio humming quietly in the background.

For sweets, **Panadería Dorada** offers fresh-baked pastries daily, including *queques secos* (buttery dry cakes) and *pan de yuca* (chewy cassava bread). Everything is baked on-site, and many regulars buy by the dozen to share with family. Most items go for under 800 colones (around $1.50 USD).

And while traditional food holds its place, Heredia's younger crowd is adding flavor to the scene with **budget-friendly fusion joints**. Small burger shops using local beef and handmade buns, taco stands run by Venezuelan immigrants, even vegan options featuring plantain-based empanadas — Heredia's food culture is growing, not gentrifying.

No matter where you eat, the common thread is sincerity. Meals are served with pride, not performance. Prices are fair. Flavors are bold. And whether you're dining beside a teenager with earbuds or an abuela in a floral apron, the feeling is the same — you belong here.

Heredia doesn't put on a show. It simply *is*. And that, perhaps, is its greatest luxury.

Outside the downtown bustle, the **neighborhoods of San Francisco and Mercedes Norte** offer a different culinary rhythm — quieter, more residential, but just as flavorful. Here, you'll find street vendors who set up in the same corner every afternoon, grilling skewers of *pinchos* (meat kebabs) or flipping handmade *tortillas palmeadas* on portable griddles. It's not unusual for locals to grab a snack on the way home from work, exchanging gossip while waiting for their food wrapped in wax paper and humility.

Perhaps the best expression of Heredia's affordable food scene is the way it *intersects with everyday life*. Food isn't a scheduled activity. It's part of the flow — something that happens on the way to the post office, after a soccer match, or between classes. You don't plan to eat well here — you just do.

For those willing to explore beyond the immediate urban sprawl, the **rural outskirts of Heredia province** introduce a more traditional, agrarian version of Tico hospitality. In **San Isidro de Heredia**, only about 20 minutes from the city center, small farms sell fresh cheese, fruits, and homemade jams from roadside stands. Family-run restaurants offer *olla de carne* — a rich beef stew with root vegetables — served in ceramic bowls on wooden tables facing the hills. Here, the air feels cleaner, time seems slower, and the prices remain delightfully low.

The **sustainability culture** is also quietly influencing the food scene. In recent years, a handful of **farm-to-table projects** have emerged — not trendy or performative, but genuinely integrated into community life. One such example is *Finca Orgánica La Flor,* a cooperative farm just north of Heredia that occasionally hosts pop-up dinners and cooking classes in an open-air kitchen. The meals are communal and rustic, with ingredients grown just a few meters away — kale, malanga, sugarcane, and herbs you might not recognize but will remember long after.

Even the city's bakeries and corner stores reflect this ethos. Walk into *Panadería Lila,* a family-run shop open since the

1970s, and you'll see generations of locals buying the same afternoon treats: *empanadas de frijol*, *tamal asado*, and *bizcochos* (spiced corn rings). The cashier greets customers by name. The scent of cinnamon, toasted cheese, and flour clings to the air. A single coin can still buy something sweet.

almuerzo corriente

But perhaps nothing embodies budget-friendly satisfaction in Heredia like **the almuerzo corriente** — the daily lunch special offered by almost every soda and small café. For under 3,000 colones (about $5.50 USD), you get a full plate: rice, beans, salad, your choice of protein (fish, chicken, pork), a fresh fruit drink, and sometimes even dessert. It's simple, nutritious, and comforting in a way that makes you feel like someone is taking care of you.

For travelers on a budget, Heredia is a gift. It doesn't ask you to compromise. Instead, it invites you to eat with the locals, spend wisely, and leave full — not just in the stomach, but in the experience. Whether you're seated at a no-name soda or standing at a roadside cart at sunset, what you're tasting is not just food — it's identity, preserved through tradition, passed through hands that never left the province, and served without pretense.

There's no need to chase authenticity in Heredia. It's already there, simmering in a pot, waiting for someone curious enough to stop and take a bite.

Chapter 8: Limón & the Caribbean Coast

"The soul of Costa Rica dances to a Caribbean beat in Limón."
— Local proverb shared by a Tortuguero guide

Costa Rica's eastern edge is often the last place travelers visit—but for many, it becomes the most unforgettable. The **Limón Province**, which stretches along the Caribbean coast from the **Nicaraguan border** to the edge of **Panamá**, is a world apart from the polished resorts of Guanacaste or the tourist-packed avenues of San José. It moves slower, pulses deeper, and speaks in a rhythm that blends **Afro-Caribbean heritage, jungle wilderness, and**

ocean breeze. This isn't the Costa Rica of curated Instagram feeds—it's the Costa Rica that locals protect and return to, again and again.

8.1 Afro-Caribbean Flavor & Rhythms

Limón's cultural identity is rooted in the strength and resilience of its **Afro-Caribbean community**, whose ancestors arrived from Jamaica and other Caribbean islands in the 19th century. Initially brought to work on banana plantations and in railway construction, these communities brought with them **language, music, religion, food, and a fierce sense of place** that still defines the region today.

Unlike the rest of Costa Rica, where Spanish dominates, **Limón speaks both Spanish and a Creole English** known locally as Mekatelyu (a twist on "Make I tell you"). Walk the central promenade in **Puerto Limón**, and you'll hear reggae spilling from open doors, smell jerk chicken grilling in roadside stands, and feel a pace that feels closer to Kingston than to San José.

The **annual Carnival in Limón city**, held in October, is the province's most vibrant cultural event. It's not a manufactured festival but an explosion of local pride. Expect all-night street dancing, parade floats swaying under the sun, calypso and soca echoing through the streets, and food stalls serving fried plantains, coconut rice, and saltfish. It's chaotic, hot, and undeniably alive.

Limón isn't just multicultural—it's proudly **anti-commercial**. The region has resisted large-scale tourism, choosing instead to honor its **communal, spiritual, and ecological values**. Travelers here are guests, not consumers—and that mindset, for many, is what makes the experience unforgettable.

8.2 Tortuguero & Cahuita National Parks

Few places in the world feel as remote—or as hauntingly beautiful—as **Tortuguero National Park**. Accessible only by **boat or light aircraft**, this protected reserve is a labyrinth of canals, lagoons, and jungle corridors that stretch along the Caribbean coast like green veins. Most visitors arrive from **La Pavona or Moín** by boat, gliding past caimans, monkeys, and sloths as they approach the village of Tortuguero, a place without cars or paved roads.

The park is famous for one thing above all: **sea turtles**. From **July to October**, thousands of **green sea turtles** return to the black sand beaches to nest, a spectacle that draws conservationists and quiet-footed tourists alike. **Nighttime guided walks** are essential during nesting season, and they're strictly regulated to protect the animals. Don't expect luxury here. Lodging in Tortuguero is simple, often rustic, and built to coexist with the natural surroundings.

Further south, **Cahuita National Park** offers a contrasting, but no less enchanting experience. It's one of the few national parks in Costa Rica where **entrance is donation-based**, managed in part by local communities rather than federal tourism authorities. The park's main draw is its **coral reef**—one of the largest and most intact on the Caribbean side. Snorkeling tours here reveal **parrotfish, stingrays, and nurse sharks** drifting silently through the warm, shallow waters.

What makes Cahuita especially magical is its balance. The jungle trail that follows the coastline weaves through **howler monkey territory**, past **tree boa sightings**, and opens onto pristine beaches like **Playa Blanca**—where the white sand glows under Caribbean sun. The town of **Cahuita** itself is small, reggae-soaked, and friendly in that way that makes you linger longer than you planned.

8.3 Wildlife Watching & Coastal Relaxation

This stretch of Costa Rica offers one of the most **biodiverse yet laid-back wildlife experiences** in Central America. **Limón's coast** teems with life, and the proximity between forest and ocean means you'll spot animals in places you wouldn't expect. **Capuchin monkeys** drink from coconut husks in hotel courtyards. **Three-toed sloths** nap in almond trees above beach cafés. **Toucans and scarlet macaws** glide over hammock-strung hostels at dawn.

Jaguar Rescue Center

The best wildlife experiences often come unplanned. Take the **Jaguar Rescue Center** in **Puerto Viejo de Talamanca**—a facility that rehabilitates injured and orphaned wildlife. Though the name evokes big cats, you're more likely to encounter **baby sloths, anteaters, and**

parrots, each with a story that speaks volumes about the relationship between nature and human impact.

Playa Cocles

Playa Chiquita

Want to relax instead of roam? **Playa Cocles**, just minutes from Puerto Viejo, offers surfing and sunbathing without the pretension of bigger surf towns. Further down, **Playa Chiquita** and **Playa Punta Uva** feel more like **tropical secrets**—small coves with clear water, calm waves, and the occasional beachside yoga class. These aren't built-up resort strips. You'll find **wooden bungalows, hammocks tied between sea grapes**, and maybe a reggae beat drifting on the breeze. It's paradise without a price tag.

Playa Punta Uva

8.4 Caribbean Cuisine & Beachfront Lodges

Costa Rican food across the country tends to follow a familiar pattern—rice, beans, plantains, chicken. But in Limón, **Caribbean flavors rewrite the menu.** Meals here are soaked in coconut milk, fired with scotch bonnet peppers, and seasoned with history.

The dish you'll hear about first is **rice and beans**—not to be confused with the national *gallo pinto*. In Limón, rice and beans are cooked in coconut milk and served with **jerk chicken, fried fish, or stewed beef**, often accompanied by fresh plantains and *patí* (spiced meat pastry). **Rondon**, a fish and root vegetable stew, is the province's most soulful dish, made with whatever the cook can "run down" that day.

Rondon

If you're in **Puerto Viejo**, try:

Selvin's (Playa Cocles) – A legendary local spot for rondon and grilled fish, with mains averaging $10–$15.

Koki Beach – Caribbean fusion meets beachfront elegance; seafood entrées run $15–$25.

Tamara's – Unassuming, deeply local, and generous in portions. A full plate of rice and beans with chicken can cost as little as $7.

When it comes to accommodations, **beachfront options in Limón are charmingly rustic or bohemian-chic**, rather than cookie-cutter luxury. Expect wooden cabinas, outdoor showers, and natural ventilation in many places.

Top picks:

Le Cameleon Boutique Hotel (Playa Cocles): Contemporary, lushly designed with jungle views and beach access. Rates: $200–$300 per night.

Le Cameleon Boutique Hotel

Casa Viva

Casa Viva (Playa Chiquita): Eco-lodge with treehouse-style rooms, outdoor kitchens, and a focus on sustainability. Rates: $120–$180.

Hotel Banana Azul (north of Puerto Viejo): Adults-only, beachfront property with handcrafted wooden décor and open-air dining. Rates: $90–$160 depending on the season.

Hotel Banana Azul

Rocking J's (budget): A backpacker legend with hammocks for rent, murals on every wall, and beach access for under $20/night.

Whether you're in the mood for fine dining with your feet in the sand or coconut curry in a tin-roof shack with plastic chairs, Limón serves its soul on a plate.

Chapter 9 Puntarenas & Nicoya Peninsula

9.1 Monteverde Cloud Forest

"In every walk with nature, one receives far more than he seeks." — **John Muir**

Perched high along the spine of Costa Rica's Tilarán Mountain Range, the Monteverde Cloud Forest doesn't announce itself with the brash drama of active volcanoes or beach sunsets. It whispers. Mist curls around the branches of ancient trees, epiphytes cling to every surface, and the forest floor—dark, rich, and always damp—teems with life you won't see unless you pause long enough for the forest to reveal itself. At around 1,440 meters (4,724 feet) above sea level, this is one of the rarest ecosystems on Earth: a cloud forest, where persistent low-level cloud cover helps support nearly 2.5% of the planet's biodiversity in just one small corner of Costa Rica.

Monteverde isn't just a nature destination; it's a philosophy of balance. It's where science, eco-tourism, and rural Costa Rican culture co-exist—sometimes uneasily, but often beautifully. Founded in the 1950s by American Quakers fleeing military conscription, the community evolved into a model of conservation-led tourism. The Monteverde Cloud Forest Reserve opened to the public in 1972 and now protects over 26,000 acres of cloud forest, drawing birders, botanists, and backpackers from across the world.

A Place That Breathes

The moment you enter the reserve, there's a palpable shift. The air becomes cooler, heavier, and filled with the scent of wet moss and wood. Monteverde averages about 3 meters (almost 10 feet) of rain annually, which is what sustains its astonishing biodiversity. You'll find more than 100 species of mammals, 400 species of birds, 120 species of amphibians and reptiles, and over 2,500 plant species—including the rare, ghostlike orchids that hide along the trails like shy sentinels.

The elusive resplendent quetzal, once sacred to the Maya, is a major draw. Local guides know the trees they favor, particularly during nesting season between March and June. But the forest rewards more than just birdwatchers. Night tours reveal kinkajous, armadillos, and glowing fungi. If you're lucky, a sloth might make a cameo—albeit a slow and silent one.

Monteverde is not a "drive-by" experience. You walk it. You listen. You let your steps grow slower, not because the trail demands it (although some do), but because the forest does.

Entry and Trails

The Monteverde Cloud Forest Biological Reserve opens daily from 7:00 AM to 4:00 PM. Tickets cost approximately **$25 USD for adults**, **$12 for students**, and **$8 for children**. You can hire a certified naturalist guide at the entrance for around **$20–$30 per person**, and doing so is highly recommended—many of the forest's best features are microscopic, or camouflaged in ways only a seasoned eye can uncover.

Popular trails include the Sendero Bosque Nuboso (Cloud Forest Trail), which meanders through dense vegetation and leads to a suspended bridge, offering a treetop view that feels like stepping into the lungs of the Earth. For a slightly longer walk, the Camino Trail leads you to "La Ventana" (The Window), a lookout where, on a clear day, the Gulf of Nicoya glimmers faintly on the horizon.

Bring waterproof everything: jackets, boots, camera cases, even notebooks. The forest is always wet, even when it isn't raining.

Sustainability, Not Just a Buzzword

Unlike many popular destinations that struggle with over-tourism, Monteverde has embraced its role as a steward of conservation. Local lodges contribute to research, and many tours directly fund preservation efforts. Even the trash bins along the trails are divided for compost, recycling, and waste—proof that sustainability here isn't a tourist-friendly label; it's a lived value.

Monteverde is also home to the **Monteverde Institute**, an international research hub offering community-based educational programs and ecotourism leadership. Some travelers even volunteer short-term, helping with wildlife monitoring or reforestation projects.

Getting There

Monteverde is accessible via a two- to four-hour drive from San José or Liberia, depending on weather and traffic. Roads have improved, but the final stretch is still a bone-jarring reminder that paradise often comes with potholes. From Route 1 (Interamericana), you'll veer off at the town of Sardinal, then wind your way up into the highlands.

If you're not renting a car, shared shuttles run daily from San José, La Fortuna, and the Pacific Coast for around **$55–$70**

USD per person. Public buses from Puntarenas are also available but far slower and less comfortable.

Where to Stay: Lodges in the Mist

Staying in Monteverde can feel like an extension of your forest immersion. Many lodges are nestled among the trees, offering views of the valley or treetop canopies.

Hotel Belmar (Rooms from **$190–$350/night**): A sustainable luxury lodge with its own microbrewery, yoga deck, and farm-to-table dining. Solar panels, composting systems, and on-site nature trails elevate the experience.

Monteverde Lodge & Gardens (From **$180/night**): Known for its glass-walled lounge overlooking butterfly gardens and thick jungle. It's mid-range in price but offers luxury in experience.

Monteverde Lodge & Gardens

Camino Verde B&B (From **$75/night**): A backpacker favorite that doesn't skimp on service or views. Offers simple, clean rooms with panoramic balcony vistas.

Selina Monteverde (From **$50–$80/night**): A co-living space popular with digital nomads, offering dorms and private rooms, coworking, yoga, and communal cooking.

Selina Monteverde

High season (December to April) sees prices spike and availability shrink—booking at least 6–8 weeks ahead is wise.

Food in the Forest

Don't expect a culinary capital, but do expect fresh, locally sourced comfort. Places like **Sabor Tico**, **Tico y Rico**, and **Orchid Coffee** offer hearty casados (plates of rice, beans, salad, plantains, and protein), fresh trout, and locally grown coffee. Restaurants here pride themselves on sustainability: organic greens from gardens behind the kitchen, dairy from Monteverde cows, and cheese made the same day it's served.

9.2 Surf Towns — Santa Teresa, Mal País, Montezuma

There's a kind of freedom in these coastal towns that you don't find in the structured confines of resorts or the polished paths of tourist hubs. Down dusty roads where barefoot travelers ride motorbikes with surfboards strapped to the side, and howler monkeys call from almond trees overhead, you'll find the soul of the Nicoya Peninsula. Santa Teresa, Mal País, and Montezuma aren't just surf towns — they are a state of mind, a rhythm of life that blends ocean, jungle, and just enough rebellion to make everything feel alive.

These three towns sit along the southern edge of the Nicoya Peninsula, one of the world's five Blue Zones — regions where people live measurably longer and healthier lives. Perhaps it's the salt air, or the simplicity, or the lack of urgency that defines time here. Whatever it is, these towns don't just host travelers. They absorb them, slow them down, and invite them to stay.

Santa Teresa: The Pulse of the Peninsula

Once a sleepy fishing village, Santa Teresa has transformed over the last decade into Costa Rica's surf-boho capital. It's gritty and glamorous in equal measure. On one side of the unpaved main road, you'll find yoga studios, fusion cafes, and luxury villas with infinity pools. On the other, you'll see dust-covered 4x4s, surfer hostels, and roadside ceviche stands in tin-roofed shacks.

But it all works. The waves are the great equalizer.

Santa Teresa's main beach stretches wide and long, with consistent swells that attract surfers year-round. Beginners can book lessons with any of the dozens of local surf schools for about **$60–$80 USD per session**, while seasoned surfers will find the early mornings and late afternoons offer ideal conditions, particularly from **May to October** when the southern swells roll in heavy.

Despite its growing popularity, Santa Teresa still feels wild. Don't expect sidewalks or street signs. Power outages are part of life, and no one is in a hurry — including the Wi-Fi. But there's magic in its disconnection. Sunsets are a town-wide ritual, with people spilling onto the sand barefoot and beer in hand, watching the horizon burn orange.

Lodging here ranges widely:

- Budget travelers often stay at places like **Selina Santa Teresa ($30 for dorms, $90+ for private rooms**), a social spot with coworking spaces and daily events.
- Mid-range charm is found at **Casa Zen Guesthouse**, starting around **$70/night**, with yoga decks and tropical gardens.
- Those craving privacy and polish might book a beachfront villa at **Latitude 10** or **Nantipa**, where

rates begin around **$400–$600 per night** depending on season and style.

Selina Santa Teresa

Casa Zen Guesthouse

Latitude 10

Dining is a highlight in Santa Teresa. **The Bakery** serves some of the best coffee and pastries in town, while **Katana** offers Asian-Latin fusion under hanging lights and open skies. Seafood, as expected, is the mainstay, often grilled simply and served with tropical fruit salsas or house-made chimichurri. Most meals fall between **$12 and $25**, though high-end restaurants can climb much higher.

The Bakery

Mal País: The Quiet Neighbor

Just a short drive — or walk, if you don't mind the heat — south of Santa Teresa, Mal País is the quieter, less commercial sibling. Think more jungle, less nightlife. Where Santa Teresa leans toward yoga and espresso, Mal País clings to its fishing village roots. Boats still dot the coves, and mornings start with the scent of salt and fresh catch.

The beach here is rockier, with tide pools and black volcanic stones carving a rugged beauty into the shoreline. Surfing is still a draw, but it's more local, less crowded. The pace is slower, more introspective. For travelers looking to step out of the buzz without leaving the ocean, Mal País is ideal.

One of the highlights here is the **Cabo Blanco Nature Reserve**, Costa Rica's first protected area, located just a few kilometers to the south. Trails wind through old-growth forests and end at remote, empty beaches. The reserve is a reminder of what Costa Rica was before tourism — and what it still protects.

Cabo Blanco Nature Reserve

Mal País offers more boutique stays than hostels. **Moana Lodge** and **Vista de Olas** offer sunset-facing rooms for **$150–$300 per night**, depending on season. Most accommodations here emphasize harmony with nature: outdoor showers, open-air lounges, and no air conditioning — not because it's lacking, but because the breeze is enough.

Dining here is quieter but personal. Family-run sodas serve casados for **$6–$10**, and beachside grills offer grilled mahi-mahi or red snapper straight from the boat to your plate.

Montezuma: The Hippie Soul

On the other side of the peninsula lies Montezuma, accessible by a bumpy, beautiful drive from Santa Teresa, or a ferry ride to Paquera followed by a drive south. Montezuma feels like a relic of another era — barefoot bohemians, dreadlocked drummers on the beach, street performers with fire sticks, and artists selling jewelry made from sea glass and coconut shells.

The town sits at the meeting point of forest and sea. One minute you're walking past murals and hammocks, the next you're on a trail into the jungle toward cascading waterfalls. The most famous — **Montezuma Falls** — is a must-visit, with three tiers of pools and the chance to cliff jump (though caution is advised). The trail begins just outside town, and entry is free, though locals may offer guided access through the "back way" for a tip.

Playa Grande

Beaches here are wilder than in Santa Teresa. **Playa Grande**, a 20-minute hike north, is a stunning crescent of golden sand and turquoise water. You'll rarely share it with more than a few others. The vibe is solitary, even romantic.

Montezuma is budget- and backpacker-friendly, with plenty of hostels and low-key eco-lodges. **Luz en el Cielo Eco B&B**, for example, offers dorms and private rooms from **$35 to $120/night**, with jungle views and organic breakfast included. At the higher end, **Ylang Ylang Beach Resort** sits nestled in a palm grove just steps from the ocean, with prices ranging from **$180 to $300 per night**.

The food scene here is eclectic. You'll find falafel stands, smoothie bars, beachfront tacos, and vegan bakeries all within a few blocks. It's easy to eat well for **under $10**, though candlelit dinners on the beach may tempt you into spending more — and rightly so.

9.3 Wellness Resorts & Yoga Retreats

In the Nicoya Peninsula, wellness isn't a curated luxury—it's a way of life shaped by climate, clean food, slow living, and deep connection to nature. This region, one of the world's five Blue Zones, has become a magnet for those seeking more than a vacation. It draws travelers craving stillness, personal renewal, or a shift in how they live entirely. Yoga isn't a trend here; it's part of the daily rhythm, often practiced outdoors beneath a thatched roof or facing a tangerine-colored Pacific horizon.

Wellness resorts throughout Puntarenas and Nicoya don't follow a one-size-fits-all formula. Some are jungle hideaways offering intimate retreats and detox programs, others are barefoot-luxury sanctuaries with spa menus and silent mornings. Whether you're drawn to sound healing under the stars, guided breathwork, or simply watching the sunset with intention, this region delivers with substance and serenity.

1. Anamaya Resort – Montezuma

Perched above Montezuma with sweeping views of the Pacific, **Anamaya Resort** blends yoga, sustainability, and personal transformation into a curated, all-inclusive retreat experience. The setting feels remote—cliffside bungalows surrounded by jungle—but the experience is fully structured.

Their flagship **Yoga & Adventure Retreats** run weekly and include daily yoga (usually two sessions a day), organic meals, excursions (like waterfall hikes or surfing), and optional workshops on nutrition, intention-setting, or astrology. The food here is all organic and often plant-based, served in communal dining areas with a panoramic view of the sea.

Prices range from **$1,295 to $2,695 USD per week**, depending on room type (shared or private) and season. The price includes all meals, most activities, and yoga classes. Spa treatments, specialty workshops, and airport transfers are extra.

Anamaya's charm is its complete immersion. No drop-ins, no day-trippers—just a group of 20–30 guests at a time, unplugging and connecting deeply with their bodies, food, and environment. It's particularly popular with solo travelers and digital detoxers.

2. Pranamar Villas & Yoga Retreat – Santa Teresa

Located directly on the shores of Santa Teresa, **Pranamar Villas** is one of the peninsula's premier wellness-focused beachfront properties. The resort features Balinese-style villas surrounded by tropical gardens, a lagoon-like pool, and an open-air yoga shala that hosts daily classes and frequent guest instructors from around the world.

Unlike some retreat centers, Pranamar functions both as a boutique hotel and a yoga destination. Guests can join individual yoga classes (**$15–$20 USD per class**) or book specialized **Yoga Vacation Packages**, which include lodging, breakfast, and daily yoga. Retreat weeks with visiting teachers range from **$1,800 to $3,200**, depending on duration and package type.

What sets Pranamar apart is its ability to straddle the line between high-end relaxation and meaningful practice. After your vinyasa flow, you can sip a fresh coconut poolside or book a deep-tissue massage using locally made oils in their serene spa pavilion. The restaurant, **Bodhi Tree**, serves organic, locally sourced fare with gluten-free and vegan options in abundance.

3. The Sanctuary at Two Rivers – Cabuya (Near Montezuma)

For travelers seeking total immersion in wellness and nature, **The Sanctuary at Two Rivers** offers a truly off-the-grid experience. Located in the small town of Cabuya, a short drive from Montezuma, this eco-resort is set on a 40-acre tropical forest reserve. It is completely solar-powered, 100%

vegetarian, and intentionally disconnected from modern distractions.

Here, days begin with jungle symphonies and sun salutations, and end with candlelit vegan dinners and deep rest. Guests stay in open-air treehouse villas that sit elevated above the forest floor. The design is minimalist but beautiful—think floating decks, meditation nooks, and outdoor rainfall showers.

Sanctuary programs are all-inclusive week-long retreats focused on yoga, meditation, cleansing, and Ayurvedic principles. Prices start at **$2,195 USD per week**, covering accommodation, three gourmet plant-based meals daily, daily yoga and meditation classes, and select excursions. They also offer teacher trainings and seasonal detox weeks.

This is not a casual wellness getaway; it's a transformative experience for travelers ready to step away from the digital world and deepen their practice.

4. Florblanca Resort – Santa Teresa

For those looking to combine luxury with wellness without the structure of a retreat schedule, **Florblanca** is a refined sanctuary on the north end of Santa Teresa. It's one of the area's most established upscale resorts, favored by honeymooners, creative professionals, and those who value privacy.

Yoga classes are offered daily in an open-air pavilion facing the ocean, and private sessions are available upon request. The in-house **Spa Bambu** offers massages, body scrubs, and facials using organic, Costa Rican ingredients. There's no required agenda here—you can design your own rhythm of rest, whether that includes surfing, Pilates, yoga, or simply reading in a hammock all afternoon.

Villa prices start around **$425 USD per night** and can exceed **$1,000/night** for premium beachfront options during peak season. It's not a budget stay, but for travelers prioritizing beauty, comfort, and wellness without rigidity, it's one of the finest experiences on the coast.

5. Blue Spirit Retreat – Nosara (on the Nicoya Coast)

Though slightly outside the bounds of the towns covered in 9.2, **Blue Spirit** in Nosara deserves mention due to its global reputation and influence in Costa Rica's wellness scene. It hosts week-long retreats led by some of the most renowned yoga teachers in the world, including names from Yoga Journal, Wanderlust, and Gaia.

Overlooking Playa Guiones, Blue Spirit offers retreat packages that include accommodation, three organic meals daily, twice-daily yoga or meditation classes, and optional workshops. Rooms range from shared eco-cabins (**$1,400/week**) to ocean-view suites (**$3,500+/week**).

The food is Ayurvedic-inspired, and the schedule allows time for surfing, beach walks, spa treatments, and reflection. Many come here for deep healing, spiritual work, or personal reset.

Wellness in the Nicoya Peninsula isn't boxed into five-star branding or new-age posturing. It lives in the slow preparation of a breakfast made from local papaya and gallo pinto, the silence you fall into after a yoga class as the ocean breathes in and out, and the willingness to trade performance for presence. Whether you're seeking a full-body detox, a spiritual reawakening, or simply the calm that comes from days with no alarm clock, the wellness offerings of Puntarenas and Nicoya are less about luxury and more about alignment.

Chapter 10: Guanacaste – Pacific Dreams and Volcanic Wilds

"The cure for anything is salt water: sweat, tears, or the sea." – Isak Dinesen

Guanacaste is more than just a province—it's Costa Rica's golden coast, a realm where the Pacific tide whispers against crescent beaches, howler monkeys call from dry forest canopies, and volcanic mud bubbles under the surface of ancient mountain ranges. With over 400 miles of shoreline, a reputation for sunshine even during the rainy season, and a unique cultural identity shaped by sabaneros (cowboys) and centuries of independence, this region draws everyone from solo wanderers to luxury seekers and surf pilgrims. Chapter 10 takes you into the heart of Guanacaste, exploring its famed beaches, opulent eco-retreats, and the rugged power of Rincón de la Vieja National Park.

10.1 Beach Escapes: Tamarindo, Playa Flamingo, Playa Conchal

Tamarindo

Tamarindo is often the first name that comes to mind when visitors think of Costa Rica's beaches. Once a sleepy fishing village, it has evolved into a vibrant town known for its easygoing surf culture, colorful sunsets, and thriving nightlife. But its charm hasn't been lost to overdevelopment—what makes Tamarindo special is its ability to serve both the novice traveler and seasoned wanderer.

The beach itself stretches for nearly two miles, its golden sand gently sloping into consistently surfable waves. Early mornings bring out the yogis and joggers, while midday sees surf schools dotting the shore, their instructors guiding eager beginners into peeling waves. Come evening, the beachfront morphs into a social hub, with music floating out from rooftop bars and bonfires flickering on the sand.

Despite its energy, Tamarindo hasn't forgotten nature. The Tamarindo Wildlife Refuge borders the town, offering kayaking and birdwatching through estuaries thick with mangroves. Leatherback turtles occasionally nest here, and locals are quick to point out conservation projects that protect these ancient mariners.

Playa Flamingo

A short drive north leads to Playa Flamingo, which earns its name from the soft blush tone that the white sand reflects during certain hours of the day. It's quieter than Tamarindo—no thumping beach bars or street vendors here—but what it offers is a kind of barefoot elegance. Yachts bob in the bay, and the surrounding hills are dotted with upscale villas and resorts. Flamingo's bay is one of the best launching points for deep-sea fishing, sailing, and scuba diving, especially at the nearby Catalina Islands, where manta rays and white-tip reef sharks glide beneath the surface.

Playa Conchal

A little farther up the coast, Playa Conchal might just be the crown jewel of Guanacaste's beaches. Unlike the grainy sands of most beaches, Conchal's shore is made up of millions of crushed seashells, giving the water a rare, crystalline glow. It's a beach that almost doesn't look real—perfect for snorkeling, swimming, or simply lying back and watching the occasional iguana scuttle by.

During the high season, luxury seekers often book into the Westin Reserva Conchal or the W Costa Rica, both of which offer seamless beach access and curated nature experiences. Yet for those looking to escape the high price tag, nearby Brasilito provides a local, budget-friendly base with easy walking access to Conchal.

10.2 Eco-Luxury Stays & Sunset Spots

One of the defining features of Guanacaste is its ability to marry raw natural beauty with comfort. While backpackers will always find hostels and cabinas across the coast, the region has also developed a reputation for some of the most thoughtfully designed eco-luxury resorts in Central America.

In Tamarindo, **Capitán Suizo Beachfront Boutique Hotel** sits beneath palm trees just steps from the sand. Constructed with sustainability in mind, its architecture uses local hardwoods, open-air breezeways, and solar energy systems. Nightly rates average between **$290–$420 USD**, depending on the season and suite type. Guests often report howler monkeys waking them at dawn—a natural alarm clock unique to Costa Rica.

Playa Dante

Further up the coast in Playa Danta, **Las Catalinas** has become a beacon of new-wave travel living. This car-free community integrates luxury villas, boutique hotels, and artisan shops into a walkable layout that embraces sustainability without sacrificing indulgence. Properties like **Casa Chameleon** offer sweeping ocean views and private plunge pools for around **$400–$600 USD per night**, drawing couples seeking a peaceful escape where the sunsets stretch like a slow-moving painting over the Pacific.

Casa Chameleon

Playa Avellanas

Drift Away Eco Lodge

At Playa Avellanas, just a short hop from Tamarindo, **Lola's** is both a beachfront institution and a lifestyle. Though not a hotel, it captures the essence of Guanacaste's rustic charm. Travelers who choose to stay nearby often book eco-lodges like **Drift Away Eco Lodge**, where solar power, organic breakfasts, and refillable water stations are part of the experience. Prices hover around **$120–$160 USD per night**.

And for the purest sunset experiences? Locals will tell you that the best views aren't always from the beach. Some of the most magical evenings are found inland, atop the low ridges near Playa Flamingo or the hills behind Conchal, where horseback tours offer golden hour rides through pastures and forest clearings. At **The Sunset Lounge**, perched above Playa Potrero, sundown cocktails come with panoramic views and a soft breeze that carries the scent of ocean salt and tropical flowers.

Notably, Guanacaste's resorts are increasingly offering "eco-certifications" that reflect their commitment to environmental stewardship. From banning single-use plastics to restoring native vegetation, this isn't greenwashing—it's a deliberate move to preserve what makes the region so magnetic.

10.3 Rincón de la Vieja Adventures

Just an hour inland from Liberia's international airport, Rincón de la Vieja National Park feels like an entirely different country. Gone are the beaches and surfboards—in their place, you'll find volcanic fumaroles, hot springs, and dense jungle trails teeming with exotic birds and howler monkeys. The park spans over 34,000 acres and centers around the massive Rincón de la Vieja volcano, a stratovolcano still very much alive beneath the surface.

Hiking here is not a gentle stroll. The **Las Pailas trail** lives up to its name—"the cauldrons"—with bubbling mud pots, steam vents, and sulfur-rich hot springs offering a kind of natural theater that feels almost otherworldly. Trekking deeper into the park leads to **La Cangreja waterfall**, a turquoise plunge pool at the end of a 10-kilometer trail that winds through dry forest and shady ravines.

La Cangreja waterfall

Adventure outfitters in the nearby town of Curubandé organize full-day experiences combining horseback riding, tubing down Rio Negro's rapids, and ziplining through forest canopies. Prices for a full-day adventure package, including lunch and park entry, typically range from **$90–$130 USD per person**. It's a day that leaves even thrill-seekers exhausted in the best way.

Rio Negro Hot Springs

For those craving relaxation after the adrenaline rush, the **Rio Negro Hot Springs**, nestled at the foot of the volcano, offer thermal pools fed directly by geothermal waters. Smearing yourself with volcanic mud before dipping into the springs is practically a rite of passage here—locals swear by its skin-healing properties.

Hacienda Guachipelín

Nearby eco-lodges like **Hacienda Guachipelín** provide an immersive base, combining rustic charm with direct access to the park. Rooms start at around **$150 USD per night**, with on-site guides and activities tailored to both families and solo travelers.

Guanacaste isn't just about the beach—it's a symphony of landscapes, from its sun-bleached shores to its smoking volcanoes. What sets it apart is how effortlessly it invites you into each of its worlds, never forcing you to choose between luxury and authenticity, or adventure and rest.

One of the lesser-known treasures of Rincón de la Vieja is the **Sendero Escondido**, or "Hidden Trail," a loop trail veiled by thick canopy and rarely crowded. While Las Pailas is more frequented for its geothermal displays, Sendero Escondido rewards those who linger with sightings of motmots, coatis, and—if luck aligns—a shy jaguarundi slipping through the underbrush. The air here is heavy with moisture and the scent of moss and rich volcanic soil. Every step feels alive.

Local guides often emphasize the duality of the park—dry forest ecosystems on one side, lush rainforest on the other. The park straddles the continental divide, creating a distinct and rare biological environment. It's not uncommon for the weather to shift dramatically mid-hike: clear skies morphing into sudden mist, the chorus of cicadas giving way to frogs and dripping leaves. These shifts are what give Rincón its moody, mystical energy—and why it's revered not just for sightseeing, but as a place to *feel* something deeper.

If you prefer your adventure with a scientific twist, the **Rincón de la Vieja Volcano Laboratory**, operated in collaboration with the University of Costa Rica, occasionally offers public talks and tours. These are often seasonal and depend on volcanic activity, but when available, they provide rare access to seismic instruments, real-time monitoring systems, and educational insights into the geothermal dynamics beneath your feet.

For those traveling with children, a more accessible (yet equally memorable) experience can be found at **Las Hornillas**, a private geothermal park just outside the national boundary. It features safe mud baths, natural steam rooms built from stone, and bridges over smoking vents where the Earth's crust seems almost within reach. Unlike many commercialized "spa" experiences, Las Hornillas feels authentic—rural, raw, and rooted in the region's geological power.

Las Hornillas

And after the mud has dried, the boots are muddied, and your muscles pleasantly ache from exploration, few things rival the simple joy of returning to your lodge, rinsing off the minerals, and sinking into a rocking chair with a cold local beer or fresh fruit juice in hand. The sounds of distant thunder—a common occurrence even when skies are blue—serve as a reminder that this place is always alive, always changing, always ancient.

A word on safety: while Rincón de la Vieja has no current eruptive activity, it is closely monitored by local authorities. Park closures can happen with little notice due to seismic shifts or heavy rains, which can trigger landslides. It's important to check the **SINAC (National System of Conservation Areas)** website or speak to local guides the morning of your visit. Weather, too, plays a role—trail conditions can change rapidly, especially from May through October during the rainy season.

For travelers who want to linger, nearby towns like Liberia and Curubandé offer quiet evenings and local flair. Liberia, often overlooked as a simple gateway city, has its own charm—whitewashed colonial buildings, surprisingly good eateries, and a pace of life that invites wandering without an agenda. Stay long enough, and you'll start to recognize familiar faces at the bakery or fruit stand, the kind of slow familiarity that big resort towns can't replicate.

Curubandé, though smaller, is more intimate. Guesthouses and eco-lodges are family-run, often with just a handful of rooms and a communal breakfast table. If you're lucky, you'll be served homemade gallo pinto and sweet plantains by someone who has lived in the shadow of Rincón their entire life. Conversations here often turn toward the land—what the volcano was like twenty years ago, how the rain has shifted, what the birds are doing this season. These are the quiet stories that fill in the soul of a place beyond its guidebook listings.

And as night falls over Rincón de la Vieja, the stars begin to assert themselves—unpolluted, unfiltered, scattered across the sky like ash from some ancient eruption. The sounds of the forest rise and shift, from birdsong to insect hum to a distant rustle in the brush. There are no loud city lights, no honking horns, just the warm scent of the forest, the cool breath of mountain air, and the quiet comfort of knowing that you've seen a part of Costa Rica that many will never find.

Rincón de la Vieja doesn't shout for attention. It waits. And for those willing to leave the shoreline behind and head inland, it offers something more enduring than a tan or a selfie: connection, memory, and awe.

10.4 Beyond the Beaches: Inland Towns, Culture, and the Soul of Guanacaste

While the coastal towns often take the spotlight, the true identity of Guanacaste is shaped inland—far from the resorts, where ox carts still roll down dirt roads and marimba music drifts from open-air community centers. This is where the region's spirit reveals itself most clearly: in its cowboy heritage, its agricultural roots, and the deeply felt pride of its people, the **Guanacastecos**.

Begin with **Santa Cruz**, often called the folklore capital of Costa Rica. Located about an hour inland from Playa Tamarindo, it's a town where tradition doesn't just survive—it thrives. On weekday mornings, the central market bustles with vendors selling everything from tamales wrapped in banana leaves to handwoven hammocks dyed in earthy reds and deep indigos. Every January, Santa Cruz hosts the **Fiestas Típicas Nacionales**, a weeklong explosion of rodeos, parades, traditional bull riding (where the bull, not the rider, is the star), and food stalls offering regional specialties like **chicharrón, tortillas palmeadas**, and fresh **cuajada cheese**.

Unlike much of Costa Rica, which leans heavily on its Spanish colonial roots, Guanacaste's culture carries strong indigenous Chorotega influences, particularly visible in the nearby town of **Guaitil**. Here, pottery isn't a tourist show—it's a living craft passed through generations. In workshops shaded by mango trees, artisans use techniques unchanged for centuries: local clay, natural dyes from tree bark and minerals, and slow-firing in underground kilns. Travelers can not only purchase these distinctive tan-and-black ceramics but also take short workshops that introduce them to the process, often taught by artisans whose hands have shaped clay since childhood.

As you move farther inland, the landscape shifts from dry tropical forest to savannah, especially around the **Cañas** and **Bagaces** regions. The scent of cattle and sugarcane fills the air. These towns aren't glamorous, but they're real—and for a certain kind of traveler, they offer a welcome break from curated experiences. Stay a night in a family-run guesthouse in Bagaces and you might find yourself invited to a backyard barbecue, where your hosts grill **carne asada** over an open flame, serve it with thick slices of fried plantain, and pour you a glass of **chicha**, a fermented corn drink with roots older than the Spanish conquest.

In this part of Guanacaste, **sabanero** (cowboy) culture is more than just a costume. Men wear wide-brimmed hats and carry machetes not for show, but because their lives are still closely tied to the land. Livestock, horses, and the rhythm of the seasons dictate the pace of life. Even schools and public events here often begin with the national anthem played on the **marimba**, a wooden percussion instrument now considered a national symbol, especially in this region.

One of the most rewarding day trips from Liberia or Santa Cruz is to **Lomas de Barbudal Biological Reserve**. It sees only a fraction of the tourists that flock to nearby national parks but offers extraordinary biodiversity—especially its population of rare bees, which have made it a hotspot for entomologists worldwide. Its dry forest ecosystem is an increasingly rare landscape in Central America, and for nature lovers tired of rainforest humidity, this area offers a completely different ecological experience.

Those interested in religious or architectural history might find a visit to **Nicoya**, the oldest colonial city in Costa Rica, both educational and moving. The town's **Iglesia de San Blas**, originally built in 1644, stands as a humble yet proud reminder of the early days of Spanish influence. The plaza around it serves as a gathering place for everything from youth soccer matches to senior citizens playing dominoes under the shade of giant Guanacaste trees.

Iglesia de San Blas

tamal asado

It would be a mistake to explore Guanacaste and not mention its food in fuller detail—because here, food isn't just sustenance; it's identity. Guanacastecan cuisine stands apart from the rest of Costa Rica thanks to its use of corn-based recipes and bold flavors. Dishes like **tamal asado**, a dense corn pudding baked over coals, and **arroz de maíz** (a seasoned corn-rice dish often prepared for festivals) are often homemade and rarely found in restaurants outside the region. At roadside **sodas** (small, local eateries), you'll find

olla de carne, a rich beef and root vegetable stew, and **rosquillas**, crunchy cornmeal rings that pair perfectly with a cup of **café chorreado**—coffee brewed the traditional Costa Rican way using a cloth filter.

Even street snacks carry local personality: try **cajeta de coco**, a coconut-based sweet, or **bizcochos**, cheese-flavored baked treats with a crumbly texture and just the right hint of salt. Many of these delicacies are sold in paper bags from wooden stalls outside town centers, especially on market days.

Yet even with its deep rural character, Guanacaste isn't stuck in the past. You'll increasingly find farm-to-table restaurants popping up in places like Santa Cruz and Nicoya, run by young chefs who've studied abroad and returned home to elevate regional recipes without losing their authenticity. This is the new face of Guanacaste—proud of its roots, but unafraid to innovate.

As you travel these inland routes, you'll notice that time stretches differently here. Schedules are loose, conversations are long, and no one seems to be in a rush—except maybe a farmer trying to get his herd across the road before the afternoon storm rolls in. It's this rhythm, unhurried and grounded, that stays with travelers long after they've washed off the volcanic mud or watched their last Tamarindo sunset.

This is Guanacaste in its fullest sense: a region where salt and soil, surf and saddle, volcano and village, all blend into a living, breathing mosaic of culture and landscape. For those willing to look beyond the glossy brochures, there's a richness here that no all-inclusive resort can replicate.

Part 3: Themed Experiences & Insider Guides

Chapter 11: Adventure & Nature

11.1 Hiking, Ziplining & Caving Hotspots

"Costa Rica contains 5% of the world's biodiversity in just 0.03% of the planet's landmass." — **National Geographic**

It's not a marketing line. It's a mathematical reality — and it explains why Costa Rica offers one of the most immersive outdoor experiences anywhere in the world. In a single day, travelers can trek across lava-strewn trails beneath active volcanoes, soar over forest canopies suspended by nothing but a harness and a pulley, then descend into an ancient limestone cave system teeming with underground rivers and bat colonies. This is not the kind of nature that quietly sits in the background. It *demands* your participation.

Hiking in Costa Rica: Trails with a Pulse

Hiking in Costa Rica is not about conquering peaks or collecting miles — it's about encountering life. Every rustle in the trees or flash of movement on the forest floor offers a possible glimpse of a coati, a motmot, or even a puma if you're exceptionally lucky. What makes the country's trail systems stand out is the way they're interwoven with biodiversity zones. Even short hikes reward you with sensory overload.

In the north, **Rincón de la Vieja National Park** delivers some of the most dynamic terrain on foot. The Las Pailas loop, a roughly 2.5-mile trail, circles through volcanic mud pots, fumaroles, and waterfalls, offering an otherworldly contrast between hot earth and cool canopy shade. Experienced hikers might attempt the longer summit trail to the park's namesake volcano, though it's only open seasonally and requires an early start and sound fitness.

Further south, **Cerro Chirripó**, the country's tallest peak, is a pilgrimage for serious trekkers. The climb is grueling — 12 miles of steep terrain to the summit at 12,533 feet — but those who make it are rewarded with the surreal sight of both the Caribbean and Pacific coasts on a clear morning. Bookings for this hike are tightly regulated, and reservations at the summit lodge must be made well in advance.

In contrast, **Manuel Antonio National Park** offers far gentler, family-friendly trails that never sacrifice beauty. The main loop trail is well-marked and flat, hugging white-sand beaches while offering frequent wildlife sightings. Even in peak tourist season, early morning hikes here can feel secluded and alive with bird calls, particularly near the less-visited Playa Gemelas.

Meanwhile, in the Monteverde Cloud Forest, you'll find trails wrapped in mist. The **Sendero Bosque Nuboso**, a moderate trail of about 1.9 miles, is ideal for travelers who want to move slowly and deliberately, letting the fog lift just enough to spot a resplendent quetzal among the branches or epiphytes glowing with morning dew. These forests are cool, damp, and dense — and almost eerily quiet except for the occasional distant call of howler monkeys.

Ziplining: Sky-High Adrenaline with a View

Costa Rica didn't invent ziplining, but it certainly made it famous. Originally used by biologists to study treetop ecosystems, these lines have become the signature adventure for thrill-seekers visiting the country — and for good reason.

With some of the longest and highest cables in the world, you don't just *ride* across the forest canopy; you *fly*.

Aventura Canopy Tour in Monteverde is often called the most iconic. The park's zipline system spans over 2.5 miles of cables, with 11 zip lines, a rappel, a tarzan swing, and the unforgettable "Superman" line — where you are strapped face-down and soar horizontally for over 1,500 meters, with only the forest below you. On clear days, the view extends all the way to the Pacific Ocean.

For those wanting an eco-conscious twist, **Sky Adventures** in Arenal offers an integrated experience. Here, ziplining is combined with a gondola ride and guided educational stops about forest ecology. Their equipment is modern and impeccably maintained, and the views of Lake Arenal and the volcano on a cloudless day are nothing short of cinematic.

Down on the Nicoya Peninsula, **Tamarindo's canopy tours** offer a smaller, more intimate experience — ideal for travelers who want the thrill but without the crowds. These lines may not be as high or long, but the ocean views and howler monkeys overhead give it a local charm that rivals the bigger operations.

While most zipline experiences are safe and suitable for anyone in decent physical health, travelers with a fear of heights should know: once you're clipped in and standing on a narrow platform 100 feet above the ground, turning back isn't usually an option.

Caving: The Quiet Heart of the Earth

If ziplining is extroverted and exhilarating, caving in Costa Rica is its opposite — introspective, subterranean, and humbling. The country's karst regions hold dozens of unexplored cave systems, but the most accessible and tourist-friendly is **Venado Caves**, just outside of La Fortuna.

Formed over 15 million years ago, the Venado Caves extend roughly 2,700 meters underground, with about a quarter open to guided tours. The experience is not for the faint of heart. Visitors are expected to crawl, wade, and sometimes squeeze through tight rock passages, often in pitch-dark conditions lit only by helmet-mounted lamps.

Inside, the walls glisten with mineral deposits, and strange rock formations named by guides — "The Papaya," "The Shark's Mouth" — line your path. Bats flutter overhead, and blind cavefish dart in shallow pools underfoot. Guides often pause to let the group experience total silence and darkness — a few seconds that feel infinite.

While tours are relatively safe and guides are experienced, this adventure isn't ideal for anyone with claustrophobia or physical limitations. Bring a change of clothes — you'll need it — and expect to be soaked, muddy, and thrilled by the end.

For those looking to avoid tight spaces but still explore underground wonders, **Barra Honda National Park** in Guanacaste offers a more technical caving experience with ladders and ropes — best suited for the adventurous with a decent level of fitness. Only a few caves are open to the public, and visits must be prearranged with certified park guides.

11.2 Best National Parks for Wildlife Viewing

You don't visit Costa Rica just to "see animals." You come to step into their world.

There's a reason biologists from across the globe spend their entire careers studying Costa Rica's protected areas. With over 30 national parks and nearly a quarter of the country under some form of environmental protection, this small Central American nation has become a safe haven for creatures that have vanished from other parts of the world. From rainforests and cloud forests to mangroves, savannahs, and coral reefs, each ecosystem is a living, breathing laboratory — and every visitor, knowingly or not, becomes part of that story.

Corcovado National Park: The Crown Jewel of Biodiversity

If there's one park that naturalists speak about with a mix of awe and reverence, it's **Corcovado National Park** on the

Osa Peninsula. National Geographic once called it "the most biologically intense place on Earth," and it's no exaggeration. This is one of the last remaining lowland tropical rainforests in Central America, and its remoteness has kept it wild in every sense of the word.

Here, tapirs roam freely along muddy trails, scarlet macaws screech through the treetops, and even the elusive jaguar has been spotted in the early morning mist. Monkeys — four species, including the endangered squirrel monkey — follow your path from the canopy above, and anteaters sometimes lumber across the open fields as if unaware of their celebrity status.

The park requires some commitment: it's only accessible by boat or via rugged footpaths, and overnight stays must be coordinated with ranger stations or permitted eco-lodges. But for wildlife photographers, conservationists, and serious nature lovers, there is no substitute. A hike through Corcovado feels less like a tourist outing and more like stepping into a wildlife documentary.

Tortuguero National Park: Where the Jungle Meets the Sea

On the opposite coast, **Tortuguero** presents a completely different — yet equally mesmerizing — environment. Often described as Costa Rica's version of the Amazon, Tortuguero is a water-based park: a maze of canals, wetlands, and flooded forests that can only be explored by boat or kayak. There are no roads here. Only nature, and the quiet lap of oars on the water.

The park's biggest claim to fame is its namesake — the sea turtles. Between July and October, green turtles come ashore in the thousands to lay their eggs on Tortuguero's long, dark-sand beaches. Watching a 300-pound female drag herself from the surf and methodically bury her clutch of eggs under moonlight is a near-spiritual experience.

But Tortuguero's wildlife isn't limited to turtles. Sloths cling to trees just inches from the canals. Caimans sun themselves on muddy banks. Basilisk lizards dash across the water surface like mythological creatures. It's a place where the rhythm of life moves slower, and the wildlife often comes to you.

Manuel Antonio National Park: Small but Mighty

One of the country's most visited parks, **Manuel Antonio** defies the idea that size matters. At just under 7 square kilometers, it's the smallest national park in Costa Rica — yet it's packed with accessible trails, breathtaking beaches, and more wildlife sightings than some parks ten times its size.

White-faced capuchin monkeys are the unofficial park ambassadors here. They boldly swing down to inspect backpacks, waiting for snacks (which visitors should *not* provide, no matter how charming the request). Iguanas bask on sun-drenched paths, sloths snooze in palm trees just feet above beachgoers, and raccoons and coatis sniff along the sand looking for dropped lunch scraps.

Despite the crowds, early-morning or late-afternoon visits can still feel serene. The beaches inside the park — particularly Playa Espadilla Sur and Playa Manuel Antonio — offer a rare combination of white sand, calm surf, and jungle backdrop. If you're limited on time or traveling with children, this park delivers maximum wildlife with minimal logistical hassle.

Monteverde Cloud Forest Reserve: Where the Air is Alive

Less about what you see and more about what you sense, **Monteverde** is a paradise for birders and atmospheric explorers. The cloud forest is a cool, mist-covered expanse perched on the spine of the Cordillera de Tilarán. It feels a world away from the tropical lowlands, yet it's home to over 400 species of birds, including the resplendent quetzal — perhaps the most sought-after avian sighting in all of Central America.

Guided tours here are highly recommended, not because the trails are hard to follow, but because the creatures you came to see are often hiding in plain sight. Camouflaged frogs cling to mossy branches. Brightly colored toucans perch silently above the trails. And somewhere in the underbrush, a jaguarundi might be watching you pass.

Butterflies, hummingbirds, and tree frogs are ubiquitous here, and several observation platforms allow for canopy-level viewing. On especially quiet mornings, it's not uncommon to hear — more than see — the forest breathing: the patter of droplets on leaves, the flap of wings through thick mist, the low call of a howler monkey echoing through the trees like a distant drum.

11.3 Water Adventures: Surfing, Rafting, Snorkeling, Scuba

There's no such thing as a typical day on the water in Costa Rica. This is a country where rivers rage through canyons, oceans collide with rainforests, and coral reefs shimmer beneath crystal-clear waves. Whether you prefer the thrill of carving down a Pacific swell or the serenity of drifting through a reef garden, the aquatic side of Costa Rica is as compelling as its jungles — maybe even more so.

The variety is part of what makes it extraordinary. You can surf world-class breaks in the morning, whitewater raft in the afternoon, and scuba dive with sharks and rays by sunset — all without ever leaving the country.

Surfing: From Beginner Swells to Pro-Level Waves

Costa Rica is a surfer's paradise, not just for its wave quality, but for the sheer range of surfable beaches spread across both the Pacific and Caribbean coasts. You don't have to be a pro to get in the water here. You just need a board, some sunscreen, and a willingness to wipe out a few times before catching your first real ride.

On the Nicoya Peninsula, **Tamarindo** is the undisputed beginner's mecca. The beach offers a long, forgiving break that's perfect for those just learning to balance on the board. Local surf schools are plentiful and professional, offering small-group lessons and video analysis. The town itself is lively, full of post-surf smoothie bars, gear rentals, and the kind of laid-back energy that makes you want to extend your stay.

Just south, **Playa Avellanas** and **Playa Negra** attract more advanced surfers with faster, heavier waves — and far fewer people. On any given day, you might find local pros sharing waves with international visitors, all watched over by curious iguanas sunning on the rocks.

Across the country, the **Caribbean coast** offers a different flavor. The waves at **Puerto Viejo's Salsa Brava** are fast, hollow, and powerful — ideal for experienced surfers only. This break is often called the "Costa Rican Pipeline," and it's not a nickname given lightly. Wipeouts here can be brutal, but for those who know how to handle them, the rewards are world-class.

What sets Costa Rica apart isn't just the quality of its waves — it's the access. You can wake up, step out of your cabina, and be in the water in minutes. And when you're done? There's always a fresh coconut waiting for you on the beach.

Whitewater Rafting: Power and Precision in the Wild

For many travelers, rafting in Costa Rica becomes the highlight of their trip — not just for the adrenaline, but for the raw, unfiltered beauty of the backcountry rivers. Imagine paddling through jungle-covered canyons, past waterfalls that tumble from unseen cliffs, with howler monkeys screaming overhead and mist rising from the water in the early morning sun. That's the reality here.

The **Pacuare River**, near Turrialba, is the crown jewel of Costa Rican rafting. Rated one of the top whitewater rivers in the world, it offers a mix of Class III and IV rapids that are both technical and exhilarating. But what truly sets it apart is the setting. The river cuts through deep rainforest gorges where the only signs of human presence are the rafts themselves. Multi-day trips allow you to stay at remote eco-lodges deep in the jungle, waking up to toucan calls before heading back out onto the water.

Rafting in Pacuare River

For beginners or families, the **Sarapiquí River** offers a slightly tamer but no less beautiful experience, with Class II and III rapids suitable for most ages. In the rainy season, this river picks up speed, offering a bit more thrill without pushing into dangerous territory.

Safety standards are generally high, with reputable outfitters providing helmets, life jackets, and thorough safety briefings. That said, it's crucial to choose experienced guides and go with a company that prioritizes river conditions over pushing tourists into unsafe waters.

Snorkeling and Scuba Diving: Beneath the Surface

Costa Rica's land-based beauty often overshadows its underwater world — unfairly so. The country boasts two coastlines with dramatically different personalities: the Pacific, deep and wild; the Caribbean, warm and vibrant. Both offer excellent diving and snorkeling opportunities, though in different styles.

On the **Pacific side**, **Caño Island Biological Reserve**, located off the Osa Peninsula, is one of the top scuba destinations in the country. The boat ride out is about 90 minutes from Drake Bay, and conditions can be choppy, but what waits beneath the surface is worth every minute. Divers routinely encounter reef sharks, eagle rays, sea turtles, and enormous schools of jacks. Visibility is often excellent — up to 80 feet — and the volcanic rock formations create dramatic underwater landscapes.

Farther north, the **Catalina Islands** near Playa Flamingo are known for their seasonal sightings of giant manta rays. These majestic creatures can reach wingspans of 20 feet and often glide gracefully just meters from divers. The area is also rich in tropical fish, eels, and the occasional octopus.

If you're on the Caribbean coast, **Cahuita National Park** offers perhaps the most accessible snorkeling in the country. Just offshore lies a living coral reef teeming with angelfish, parrotfish, and sea fans. Snorkeling tours often combine with boat rides and beach picnics, making for a relaxed, family-friendly outing.

One important note: coral reef health in the Caribbean has been impacted by storms and warming waters, so always choose a tour that practices responsible reef etiquette — no touching, no standing, no collecting. Costa Rica takes marine conservation seriously, and visitors are expected to do the same.

For those seeking the ultimate underwater adventure, **Bat Islands (Islas Murciélago)** in the northwest Pacific are known for more advanced dives, including bull shark encounters — no cage, just nerves and know-how. Not for beginners, but unforgettable for the qualified and brave.

Chapter 12: Eco-Tourism & Sustainability

12.1 What Makes Costa Rica a Global Leader

"We must be the change we wish to see in the world." — *Mahatma Gandhi*
In Costa Rica, that change isn't just a slogan—it's a national strategy.

By the mid-1980s, while much of the world was still debating the balance between economic development and environmental preservation, Costa Rica made a bold pivot. The country, once suffering from one of the highest deforestation rates in Latin America, began investing aggressively in conservation. Instead of following the pattern of rainforest depletion for agriculture or development, Costa Rica reversed course. Today, over 50% of the country's landmass is forested, and roughly 25% is protected in national parks and biological reserves—the highest percentage in the world for a country of its size.

This wasn't a coincidence or a convenient marketing move. It was a deliberate, deeply embedded national priority that reshaped the country's global identity. The shift was not just environmental—it was political, social, and economic. The Costa Rican government abolished its military in 1948, choosing instead to divert funding toward education, healthcare, and environmental stewardship. That decision, radical at the time, created a culture where sustainability could flourish—not only in law but in everyday life.

Costa Rica has since become a pioneer of eco-tourism not just by promoting "green travel," but by building infrastructure that makes it both accessible and meaningful. It's a place where visitors can hike through a cloud forest in the morning, release baby sea turtles at dusk, and sip shade-grown, organic coffee while learning about sustainable agriculture—all in a single day. But more importantly, they can do these things *without guilt*, knowing their dollars are often directly contributing to conservation efforts, community development, and low-impact tourism.

In 2007, the country committed to becoming carbon-neutral by 2021—a deadline it has since adjusted to 2050—but the ambition itself set a new bar for the region. And in 2019, Costa Rica generated 99.62% of its electricity from renewable sources, largely from hydropower, geothermal energy, and wind. This isn't just an environmental talking point—it's a lived experience. Even travelers feel the impact: lower emissions, cleaner air, fewer plastic bottles, more electric vehicles, and public transit routes designed with sustainability in mind.

When travelers consider eco-tourism destinations around the globe, few places offer the credibility and infrastructure that Costa Rica does. Unlike other nations where "green" travel options are limited to niche resorts or small protected zones, Costa Rica has mainstreamed it. Sustainability isn't an upgrade—it's the standard.

The result is a destination that doesn't just host tourists—it educates them. And in doing so, it inspires a more conscious type of travel.

12.2 Top Eco-Lodges & Sustainable Tours

The rise of eco-tourism in Costa Rica has transformed the way accommodations and tour operators approach business. Here, the best lodges don't just "reduce plastic" and call it a day—they integrate sustainability into every corner of the guest experience, from the materials used in construction to the sourcing of food, to how wastewater is treated.

At the heart of the Osa Peninsula, a region renowned for its biological richness, you'll find Lapa Rios Lodge—a benchmark in eco-lodging. Perched above the forest canopy and overlooking the Golfo Dulce, Lapa Rios is more than a beautiful stay. It's a conservation initiative with luxurious accommodations built entirely from locally sourced materials. The lodge funds local education, supports wildlife corridors, and employs only local residents. Guests are invited to participate in reforestation efforts, wildlife monitoring, and educational talks led by naturalists.

Similarly, Pacuare Lodge, nestled along the wild Pacuare River, blends adventure and ethics seamlessly. Only accessible by raft or zipline, the lodge is completely off-grid. It uses clean energy, sources food from an organic garden, and maintains deep partnerships with nearby indigenous communities. Yet the experience is refined—gourmet meals, candlelit rooms, and private plunge pools surrounded by untouched rainforest. It's sustainability without sacrifice.

On the Caribbean side, Selva Bananito Lodge provides another model. Here, the owner's family gave up logging rights in favor of preserving the primary forest. Guests staying here don't just observe nature—they engage with it through low-impact hikes, tree planting activities, and birdwatching excursions that support local biodiversity programs.

Beyond accommodations, Costa Rica's eco-tours are equally impactful. You can join a guided walk with the Monteverde Conservation League, where fees go directly to maintaining the cloud forest. You can kayak through the mangroves of Damas Island with a tour company certified by the Costa Rican Tourism Institute's CST (Certification for Sustainable Tourism), which ensures social, economic, and ecological responsibility.

What sets these experiences apart isn't just the "green" badge. It's the immersive, human connection. These are operations where staff members know the names of every monkey species by heart—not because it's in a brochure, but because they grew up in the forest you're now exploring.

12.3 How to Travel Responsibly

Traveling responsibly in Costa Rica doesn't require perfection—it requires awareness. In a country where sustainability is embedded into the tourism industry, many of the systems are already in place. But it's the traveler's mindset that completes the cycle.

Start with choices. Opt for accommodations that are part of Costa Rica's CST program, or that offer transparency about their practices. Look for hotels that use renewable energy, employ local staff, and avoid single-use plastics. But don't stop at the hotel—choose tour operators who reinvest in the land they use, whether through forest protection, wildlife care, or cultural preservation.

Responsible travel also means adjusting behaviors. Avoid feeding wildlife or taking flash photos of nocturnal animals. Stay on marked trails—even when the hidden shortcut looks more appealing. Support local artisans instead of imported souvenir shops. These aren't restrictions—they're actions that protect the very experience you came for.

Understanding cultural sensitivity is equally vital. Costa Rica is a nation proud of its democratic history, peaceful stance, and biodiversity. Engage with locals, ask questions, learn a few Spanish phrases—even a simple "¡Pura vida!" exchanged with sincerity can open conversations and hearts. Remember that many communities in Costa Rica have made sacrifices to preserve their ecosystems. Respect their time, space, and traditions.

Perhaps the most impactful thing travelers can do is extend their awareness beyond the trip. Costa Rica has long been a living classroom for conservation. Take the lessons home. Reduce your waste. Offset your flights. Rethink your consumer habits. The beauty of eco-travel is not just that it offers a lighter footprint—it leaves you with deeper roots.

When done right, responsible travel doesn't just protect paradise—it deepens your connection to it.

Chapter 13 Culture & Cuisine

13.1: Local Dishes to Try & Where to Find Them

"The best way to understand a country is through its kitchens."
— **Unknown traveler's proverb, scribbled on the wall of a soda in Alajuela**

There's no better entry point into the Costa Rican soul than a steaming plate of *Gallo Pinto* at sunrise, served with a slice of fried plantain and a dollop of natilla (sour cream), with the smell of strong local coffee curling through the air. Food in Costa Rica isn't just nourishment — it's a rhythm of life, a source of pride, and a quiet daily celebration of culture and history.

Many travelers arrive expecting something close to the bold spices of Mexican cuisine or the complex heat of Peruvian dishes. But Costa Rican food isn't built to impress on the first bite — it wins you over slowly, in bowls of comforting simplicity, in meals shared with families at plastic tables, and in dishes seasoned not with extravagance, but tradition.

Gallo Pinto: Breakfast at the Heart of the Nation

A deceptively simple mix of rice and beans, *Gallo Pinto* is Costa Rica's most iconic dish — and one you'll encounter in every corner of the country. But it's more than fuel; it's part of the morning ritual. Traditionally cooked with sautéed onions, bell peppers, and a generous dash of *Salsa Lizano* (a slightly tangy, Worcestershire-style condiment), it's served alongside eggs, tortillas, fried cheese, or avocado — depending on the region.

For a truly local experience, order it at **Soda Tapia**, a beloved 24-hour eatery in San José that has been dishing out pinto for generations. Or wander into **Soda Yogui's** in La Fortuna, a no-frills spot where locals, guides, and travelers crowd in before setting out for Arenal.

In coastal regions, don't be surprised if your *Gallo Pinto* has coconut milk stirred in — a nod to Afro-Caribbean influence, especially near Puerto Viejo. There, you'll find pinto that's slightly sweeter, richer, and undeniably comforting.

Casado: The Midday Plate of a Working Nation

If *Gallo Pinto* is the morning heartbeat, *Casado* is the fuel of the afternoon. The word means "married," and the dish lives up to its name: it's a marriage of rice, black beans, salad, a protein (typically grilled chicken, pork, or fish), and sometimes a fried plantain or slice of avocado.

While nearly every soda (Costa Rican diner) offers its own version, the best *Casados* come from family-run kitchens that rotate ingredients based on what's fresh. In Cartago, stop by **Soda El Molino**, where the chicken is grilled over charcoal and the beans simmer in a clay pot for hours. In Monteverde, try **Sabor Tico**, which pairs locally grown vegetables with meat from regional farms.

The brilliance of *Casado* is that it's not pretentious. There's no plating finesse, no garnish to speak of. It's practical, hearty, and deeply satisfying — especially after a hike through cloud forest trails or a morning of zip-lining.

Chifrijo: Bar Snack Turned National Treasure

You don't find *Chifrijo* on breakfast menus — it belongs to the late afternoon, the golden hour when locals unwind with friends over cold beer. This beloved dish combines crispy chicharrón (fried pork belly), black beans, fresh pico de gallo, avocado, and crunchy tortilla strips, all layered in a bowl. It's rich, indulgent, and hard to stop eating.

The best *Chifrijo* comes from bars that take their pork seriously. In San José, **Bar La Cava del Duende** is famous for theirs — served with jalapeños on the side and icy Imperials on tap. Outside the capital, head to **Bar Los Amigos** in Jacó, where the surf crowd gathers around bowls of *Chifrijo* after a long day in the waves.

A tip from the locals: add a squeeze of lime, a splash of Lizano, and don't be shy with the hot sauce. It's not just a snack. It's a ritual.

Olla de Carne: A Taste of Home in a Bowl

While less flashy than street food favorites, *Olla de Carne* is the comfort food that Costa Rican grandmothers swear by. It's a beef stew slow-cooked with carrots, chayote, plantains, yuca, and other root vegetables — a hearty, rustic dish made for Sunday family gatherings.

You'll find it mostly on weekends, especially in small mountain towns. In Zarcero, famous for its whimsical topiary garden, **Soda La Laguna** serves *Olla de Carne* with handmade corn tortillas and a warm smile. In rural Alajuela, stop at **Soda El Campesino**, where the stew simmers in a blackened pot over an open flame.

There's something grounding about eating *Olla de Carne* on a cool evening while the fog rolls in — a reminder that food, at its best, is about connection and place.

Regional Flavors: From Coast to Highlands

Costa Rica's small size belies its culinary diversity. Along the Caribbean coast, the influence of Afro-Caribbean heritage is strong. Dishes like *Rondón* — a seafood and coconut milk stew — carry the bold flavors of the region. In Limón, visit **Miss Edith's** for an unforgettable version, filled with crab, fish, green plantain, and fragrant herbs.

On the Nicoya Peninsula, known as one of the world's few Blue Zones, locals favor lighter, plant-based meals — beans, squash, corn, and fresh fruit. Here, food is often organic by default, and meals emphasize longevity as much as flavor. Restaurants like **The Natural Center** in Nosara blend traditional ingredients with a modern wellness twist.

In the northern cattle ranch regions like Guanacaste, grilled meats take center stage. Try *carne asada* or *chorizo* straight from the fire at roadside *parrilladas* — open-air BBQ spots where the smell of charred meat drifts into the jungle.

13.2: Food Markets & Street Eats

It starts with the aroma — not just one scent, but a layered, chaotic orchestra of them. Fried plantains sizzling in oil. The citrus burst of sliced guanábana. Roasted corn twisting slowly on a metal rack, its kernels blistered and sweet. Then come the sounds: vendors calling out the names of fruits in rapid-fire Spanish, the clang of knives on cutting boards, the sudden whoosh of a blender turning pineapple and mint into something cold and life-saving.

Costa Rica's food markets are not passive destinations. They're alive, defiant in their energy, and offer something that restaurants — no matter how good — never quite match: authenticity stripped of performance.

Mercado Central, San José: A Controlled Frenzy

In the heart of the capital, the **Mercado Central** sprawls like a living museum of Costa Rican daily life. Established in 1880, it's less of a tourist stop and more of a rite of passage. The narrow aisles feel like a labyrinth at first, crowded with shopkeepers selling everything from dried spices and herbal remedies to leather boots, coffee beans, and knockoff sunglasses.

But the real draw is the food — tucked into tiny stalls and communal counters where locals take their coffee standing up and gossip over midmorning snacks.

At **Soda Los Angeles**, one of the oldest in the market, the *empanadas* come hot and greasy, stuffed with cheese, beans, or beef, and always best with a spoonful of housemade *chilero* — a pickled hot pepper relish that locals don't live without. If you're lucky enough to find *arroz con leche* (rice pudding) being served fresh in the afternoon, don't pass it up.

This is where you taste Costa Rica on its own terms — no pretense, no performance, just honest food that has fed generations.

Puerto Limón's Street Corners: Caribbean Flavor in Motion

Head east to Limón and the atmosphere changes completely. The air thickens, the colors brighten, and the rhythm slows down. Along the Caribbean coast, street food isn't just sustenance — it's an extension of Afro-Caribbean heritage.

Stalls here are less formal than in the cities. Sometimes it's a table set up under a beach almond tree, other times it's a mobile grill welded to the back of a bicycle. Either way, the food is unforgettable.

Order *patí*, a flaky pastry filled with spiced beef or chicken, similar to a Jamaican patty but with a Tico twist. Or grab a serving of *rice and beans* — not to be confused with the traditional *Gallo Pinto* — cooked in coconut milk and thyme, often served with fried fish that's been marinated in lime and scotch bonnet pepper.

And if you spot a woman selling shaved ice from a hand-pushed cart, stop. Her *granizados* — layered with syrup, condensed milk, and powdered milk — are not just for children. They're a humid afternoon's best companion.

Farmers' Markets (Ferias): Fresh, Local, Unpolished

Every town in Costa Rica hosts a **feria** — a weekly farmer's market where rural vendors roll in with the best of their land. These markets are not tourist shows; they're where Tico families shop for the week, bargaining over mangos, papayas, avocados, and bundles of cilantro the size of your head.

The **Feria Verde de Aranjuez** in San José is perhaps the most cosmopolitan — here you'll find organic produce, artisanal cheeses, handmade soaps, vegan pastries, and even kombucha. But head to smaller towns like Atenas or Grecia and the feria feels more intimate: rows of imperfect fruit stacked in crates, tamales wrapped in banana leaves sold from coolers, and raw sugarcane juice pressed on-site.

Food here is affordable and plentiful. Most vendors will let you sample before you buy, and they'll explain — with genuine pride — what makes their yuca smoother or their bananas sweeter than the rest.

Bring cash, bring a reusable bag, and most of all, bring time. The feria isn't for rushing. It's for lingering, tasting, and perhaps being invited to someone's farm if you show enough interest.

Street Eats: Simple Meals, Bold Characters

Outside the formality of markets, Costa Rican streets come alive with vendors whose menus fit in their pockets and whose cooking gear fits on a tricycle.

In **Alajuela**, try the *carnitas* stand that operates late into the night behind the central cathedral — piles of chopped pork grilled with garlic, served with corn tortillas and a splash of lime. In **Liberia**, keep an eye out for the woman who sells *chorreadas* (corn pancakes) in the mornings from a cart under a jacaranda tree. She flips them fast, slathers them with natilla, and always smiles when you ask for a second one.

And if you find yourself in **Puntarenas**, stroll along the boardwalk and sample *Churchill* — an outrageous local dessert that's part snow cone, part condensed milk explosion, part carnival in a cup. It's wildly sweet, arguably absurd, and unmistakably Costa Rican.

These are not dishes you'll find listed on TripAdvisor or covered in culinary blogs. But they are the ones you'll remember — not because they were gourmet, but because they were real.

13.3: Festivals to Catch in 2025–2026

It doesn't matter how long your flight was or how much Spanish you know. When you stumble upon a Costa Rican festival — even by accident — the feeling is unmistakable: you're no longer an observer. You're part of something. The drumbeat becomes your pulse. The street food becomes your dinner. The stranger dancing beside you becomes your friend, if only for a night.

Costa Rica's festivals are less about spectacle and more about spirit. They reflect the country's mix of Indigenous traditions, Catholic rituals, Caribbean rhythms, and small-town pride. Whether you plan your trip around them or discover them by surprise, these celebrations offer rare windows into the nation's identity — one street parade or barefoot dance at a time.

Día de los Diablitos (Day of the Little Devils) – Boruca, December 31–January 2

High in the mountains of the southern Pacific, far from the resorts and highways, the Indigenous Boruca people host one of Costa Rica's most powerful and symbolic festivals. *Día de los Diablitos* isn't about fireworks or DJs. It's a three-day reenactment of the Spanish conquest, told through masks, fire, ritual combat, and communal spirit.

Masked dancers — the "little devils" — don hand-carved wooden faces painted in vivid colors, each one representing a spirit of nature or an ancestral force. They confront a costumed "bull," symbolizing the Spanish invaders. There are no grandstands. No VIP areas. Just villagers, drummers, tourists who've made the journey, and the thick, smoky air of burning herbs.

If you're looking for something authentic and untouched by commercial tourism, this is it. But be respectful. Ask before taking photos. Learn the meaning behind the masks. And if someone hands you *chicha* (fermented corn drink), sip slowly — it's stronger than it looks.

Palmares Fiestas – January (Exact 2025 dates TBD)

Picture a sleepy coffee town that transforms overnight into the biggest party in the country. That's **Palmares**, a village in the Central Valley that explodes with energy each January during its two-week fiesta. It draws half a million people — locals and travelers alike — and feels like a mashup of rodeo, street carnival, beer fest, and old-world procession.

The daily agenda is loose but reliably full: bullfights (non-lethal), horseback parades (*tope*), massive concerts, and impromptu street parties that stretch into the early hours. During the **"Carnaval"**, floats wind down the main street while brass bands keep the crowd on its feet. On the final weekend, a sky full of fireworks marks the unofficial end, though the hangovers last longer.

It's chaotic, loud, and not for the faint of heart — but if you want to see Costa Ricans celebrate *just because they can*, Palmares is the place.

Semana Santa (Holy Week) – March 30–April 5, 2025

No event blends the sacred and the sensory quite like **Semana Santa**. Held during the week leading up to Easter, it's observed across the country, but particularly in towns like **Cartago**, **Heredia**, and **San José**, where Catholic traditions run deep.

On Holy Thursday and Good Friday, the country slows down. Streets empty. Businesses close. Even buses reduce their schedules. But in select plazas, life moves in solemn procession. Hooded figures carry life-sized statues of Christ and the Virgin Mary. Children scatter flower petals. Drummers beat a steady, mournful rhythm.

For travelers, it's not the time to expect high-energy tourism. Instead, it's a moment to witness reverence on a national scale. That said, many Costa Ricans use the week for beach escapes — so coastal towns like Jacó and Tamarindo fill quickly. If you stay inland, though, you'll see a very different side of the country: reflective, spiritual, deeply rooted.

Día de la Independencia – September 15

If you're traveling through Costa Rica in mid-September, it's impossible to miss the patriotic buildup. Flags hang from every window. Schoolchildren practice traditional dances in courtyards. And on the evening of September 14, candle-lit lanterns begin to glow across the country — a tribute to the torch run that carried the news of independence in 1821.

September 15 is a full-fledged national holiday. Morning parades fill the streets with marching bands, folkloric costumes, and horses adorned in ribbons. In smaller towns, everyone knows the performers by name. In cities, it feels more like a pageant.

To catch the full spirit, visit **Alajuela** or **Cartago**, where independence pride runs deep. Find a curb, grab a cup of fresco (fruit juice), and join the crowd. There's no entrance fee, no agenda — just a whole country remembering who they are.

Carnival de Limón – Mid-October (Exact 2025 date TBA)

Costa Rica's Caribbean coast is a world of its own, and nowhere is that clearer than during **Carnival de Limón**. Held in mid-October, it celebrates the region's Afro-Caribbean culture with ten days of music, dance, food, and unfiltered joy.

Expect massive street parades, booming sound systems, and vendors frying up *patí* and *plantain tarts* on every corner. Soca and calypso dominate the airwaves. Costumes range from traditional to outrageous. And if you're lucky, you'll catch the *comparsa* troupes — groups of dancers and drummers that move with such energy, the ground practically shakes beneath them.

Limón itself isn't always polished — but during Carnival, it shines. Just book accommodations early. Rooms fill fast, and prices spike closer to the festivities.

Fiestas Patronales – Year-Round

Scattered throughout Costa Rica are dozens of **Fiestas Patronales** — local patron saint festivals that mix faith, food, and good old-fashioned fun. These aren't widely advertised or covered by travel guides, but stumble upon one and you'll never forget it.

Each town honors its patron saint with mass, followed by horse parades, live marimba music, homemade tamales, fireworks, and often an old-fashioned mechanical bull. The scale ranges from a single street fair to a town-wide holiday.

The beauty is in the spontaneity. One weekend in February, you could find yourself in **Santa Cruz**, dancing with strangers in the plaza under strings of papel picado. Another night in July, you might join a candlelight vigil in **San Ramón**, your path lit by fire and hymns. It's all part of the rhythm of Costa Rican life — unscheduled, unscripted, unforgettable.

13.4: Cooking Classes & Cultural Workshops

There's something grounding about the moment your hands meet masa dough, still warm from the mixing bowl. It doesn't matter whether you've cooked before or not — shaping a tortilla the way someone's grandmother taught them to do 50 years ago has a way of slipping past the tourist lens and straight into something far more real.

For many travelers, sightseeing is no longer enough. They want to *do*, to touch, to learn — to carry something home that doesn't fit in a suitcase. Costa Rica answers that craving with a growing network of cooking classes and cultural workshops rooted in tradition, family history, and, more often than not, a steaming plate of something delicious shared at the end.

These aren't corporate cooking schools or rehearsed performances. The best classes happen in open-air kitchens, backyard patios, or small community centers, led by locals whose knowledge isn't learned — it's inherited.

Cooking with Locals: The Heart of the Experience

In a small house near La Fortuna, just past the banana trees and down a dirt road GPS won't find, Doña Mara welcomes guests into her home with the warmth of a lifelong hostess. Her cooking class doesn't begin with knives or ingredients. It starts at the market. She insists on it.

You'll walk through the stalls with her as she explains why certain tomatoes are better for *salsa criolla*, what to look for in fresh cilantro, and why her mother never used garlic in her *Gallo Pinto*. Back in her home, you'll spend the next few hours chopping, frying, laughing, and — often without realizing it — speaking more Spanish than you thought you could.

This is the experience that so many guides don't mention: the transformation of food into a conversation, culture into muscle memory. You leave full, yes, but also connected — to the land, to a family, and to a story that never makes it onto an itinerary.

You'll find similar setups all across the country. In Monteverde, the air smells of mist and herbs in a high-altitude kitchen where guests learn to make *empanadas* from scratch. In Puerto Viejo, a cooking class might double as a dance party, where the host peppers instructions with reggae beats and spicy jokes, and you'll learn how to make coconut rice that actually tastes like the sea.

What You'll Learn (Beyond Recipes)

Cooking classes in Costa Rica often go far beyond the plate. Many incorporate history, storytelling, and cultural philosophy into the lesson. One class in the Nicoya Peninsula opens with a short presentation on the region's Blue Zone status — the rare designation given to places where people live measurably longer lives. You'll learn not just how to prepare *sopa negra* (black bean soup), but why the ingredients matter for health, community, and longevity.

In the Central Valley, some workshops start with a quick lesson on medicinal herbs used in Costa Rican households, followed by a tour of the instructor's garden. By the time you sit down to eat, you haven't just made food — you've reoriented how you think about it.

Many programs also include hands-on practice with making tortillas, tamales, plantain-based desserts, and even drinks like *agua dulce*, made by melting raw sugarcane blocks into hot water — Costa Rica's answer to comfort in a cup.

Cultural Workshops: Beyond the Kitchen

Not every traveler wants to cook, but that doesn't mean they can't dive deep into Costa Rican culture. The country's rural communities, especially those with Indigenous roots, offer a wide range of workshops designed to preserve — and share — their traditions with respect and pride.

In the mountains near Turrialba, you can spend an afternoon with members of the Cabécar tribe, learning how to weave with natural fibers harvested from the forest. These workshops aren't performances — they're collaborative sessions led by artisans who see their work not just as craft, but as cultural protection.

Elsewhere, in Guaitil — a village known for its pre-Columbian Chorotega pottery — travelers can take part in ceramic workshops that follow traditional methods. You'll dig your hands into the clay, shape a bowl or plate, and paint it using natural pigments derived from volcanic earth. Each piece carries not only the fingerprints of its maker but the silent echoes of an art form that's survived for over a thousand years.

Music, too, finds its way into these cultural experiences. In Alajuela, there are small programs where visitors can learn basic *marimba* or traditional folk dance — a joyful, feet-stomping expression of Costa Rican rhythm that comes with as much laughter as instruction.

Sustainability & Impact: Why These Experiences Matter

Most of these classes and workshops are hosted by local families, cooperatives, or community tourism initiatives. Your participation often directly supports rural economies and helps preserve cultural knowledge that might otherwise disappear under the weight of modernization.

Booking through small, local platforms — or asking your host or lodge for recommendations — ensures your money stays in the community. Avoid overly commercial tours that feel rushed or transactional. The best experiences usually come from those that aren't polished — the ones where someone's child runs through the kitchen mid-lesson, or where the tortillas aren't quite perfect, but the moment is.

Chapter 14: Digital Nomads & Remote Workers

"A laptop and a beach are not enough. The true luxury is building a life where your work and your surroundings are in sync — and Costa Rica gives you that balance without asking you to choose."

Remote work is no longer a trend — it's a transformation, and Costa Rica has stepped confidently into its role as one of Central America's most appealing destinations for digital nomads. Beyond the surface of "pura vida" beaches and vibrant rainforests lies a quietly growing infrastructure that caters to those who work from anywhere but want *somewhere* meaningful.

For remote professionals, Costa Rica offers the things that truly matter: stable internet in key regions, a network of coworking spaces, a relatively low cost of living, a supportive expat and local community, and something intangible but undeniable — a lifestyle that prioritizes well-being. Whether you're a freelance designer looking for a quiet studio in the mountains, or a software engineer coding from a café near the waves, you'll find Costa Rica welcoming — not just as a visitor, but as a temporary home.

14.1 Best Places to Live & Work

While Costa Rica is small on the map, it offers remarkably distinct environments to base yourself depending on your work style, lifestyle needs, and appetite for adventure. Some digital nomads are drawn to the city comforts of San José, while others build their lives in barefoot towns on the Nicoya Peninsula. Here's a deeper look at the country's strongest hubs for remote professionals:

San José & Escazú

The capital and its surrounding suburbs remain the most practical base for many remote workers who prioritize stability. San José isn't flashy, but it delivers. Reliable internet is easy to find, and coworking spaces like **Selina CoWork, Impact Hub,** and **Spaces** offer modern facilities and event calendars that keep you connected with fellow remote workers and entrepreneurs. The neighborhood of Escazú, in particular, has become an expat favorite — clean, modern, and just far enough from the chaos of downtown. Expect gated communities, shopping centers, and a surprisingly international food scene.

Santa Teresa

A rugged, sun-soaked paradise on the Nicoya Peninsula, Santa Teresa might just be the poster child for the surf-and-work lifestyle. This is where MacBook screens light up beneath palm-thatched roofs, and entrepreneurs take their lunch breaks barefoot in the sand. The energy here is youthful, creative, and laid-back — but don't mistake the casual vibe for laziness. Behind those hammocks and smoothie bowls are highly motivated people building startups, brands, and entire livelihoods online. Infrastructure can be inconsistent (expect power cuts during storms), but most rentals come with backup power and solid Wi-Fi. Coworking spaces like **Hustle House** and **Selina** cater directly to nomads.

Tamarindo
Once a sleepy surf town, Tamarindo has grown into a full-fledged digital nomad hub — and unlike Santa Teresa, it's a little more polished. With its paved roads, stronger tourism infrastructure, and proximity to Liberia's international airport, it's a practical and popular choice. Coworking spots are scattered through the town, including **Sand & Surf** and **Tamarindo CoWork**, both offering high-speed internet and ocean views. The nightlife here is livelier than most nomad towns, and there's a well-established expat community that supports everything from yoga groups to crypto meetups.

Puerto Viejo (Caribbean Coast)

For those who want something *different* — less influenced by North American tourism, more connected to Afro-Caribbean culture and biodiversity — Puerto Viejo delivers a rich experience. It's not as developed in terms of coworking infrastructure, but remote workers settle here for the rhythm of life, the vibrant food, and the proximity to nature. Internet can be patchy outside the town center, but short-term rentals inside the main town typically come with reliable access. The digital community here is small but passionate — and often attracts creatives, writers, and wellness professionals.

La Fortuna

Better known for volcanoes and hot springs, La Fortuna might not seem like a digital nomad destination at first glance. But it has quietly emerged as a great place for short stints. It's perfect for those who want to unplug just a little — to work mornings and spend afternoons exploring waterfalls or soaking in geothermal pools. Internet is improving in town, and several boutique hotels and Airbnbs offer strong enough Wi-Fi for video calls and light streaming. If your work doesn't demand daily Zoom meetings, this could be your mountain retreat.

14.2 Internet Access & Coworking Spots

For many remote workers, internet access is non-negotiable — and in Costa Rica, your experience will vary based on where you land. In the capital and major tourist towns, speeds are fast and stable. Fiber-optic connections are available in most parts of San José, Heredia, and Escazú, as well as in expat-heavy towns like Tamarindo and Santa Teresa.

Outside of these hubs, especially in rural or coastal regions, connections can be slower and less reliable — not unusable, but frustrating for those running video-heavy workloads. That said, Costa Rica has made impressive strides in connectivity over the last few years. In 2025, ICE (the state telecom provider) and private companies like Tigo and Kolbi continue to expand their reach with faster packages and broader fiber deployment.

Coworking spaces are not just workspaces in Costa Rica — they're social hubs. You'll find whiteboards, ergonomic chairs, quiet zones, but also hammocks, kombucha bars, and surfboards stacked by the door. Spaces like **Selina CoWork** (multiple locations nationwide), **Creaspace** in Santa Teresa, and **CoWork Café** in San José offer membership plans, day passes, and community events.

For those who prefer working from cafés, Costa Rica offers plenty of laptop-friendly spots with strong coffee and free Wi-Fi. Just be mindful of café etiquette: buy something regularly, avoid hogging space during peak hours, and don't treat every table like your office. Most places are welcoming as long as you're respectful and discreet.

SIM cards are easy to purchase at the airport or in any town. A Kolbi or Claro prepaid plan with 10GB of data costs roughly $10–15 USD and can be topped up online. This is essential for tethering during outages or working on the move.

14.3 Budgeting a Remote Life in Paradise

The image of a remote worker sipping coconut water in a hammock can be misleading. Yes, Costa Rica offers natural beauty in abundance and a slower pace of life — but for digital nomads trying to stretch their income while maintaining productivity, budgeting here requires more than optimism and postcards. Living affordably in Costa Rica is possible, but it depends heavily on your location, lifestyle, and how well you adapt to local ways of living.

Let's start with accommodation, which will likely take the largest slice of your monthly expenses. In high-demand areas like Tamarindo or Santa Teresa, prices have risen steadily. A modest one-bedroom apartment or studio near the beach can run anywhere from $700 to $1,500 USD per month, depending on amenities, season, and proximity to tourist zones. Short-term rentals through Airbnb tend to be higher, while long-term leases (often negotiated in person or through local Facebook groups) are more economical. If you're open to shared housing, coliving setups like **Outsite**, **Selina**, and **Drifter's Coliving** offer flexible contracts and come bundled with coworking access, utilities, and community events.

In less tourist-saturated towns like Grecia, Atenas, or even parts of Heredia, rental costs drop significantly — and you're more likely to find quiet, furnished apartments for under $600 a month. These inland towns also offer cooler climates and a more traditional Costa Rican experience, favored by retirees and long-term expats alike.

Food costs, as with most things in Costa Rica, depend on whether you live like a local or import your habits from home. Shopping at *ferias* (weekly farmers' markets) and cooking at home keeps costs low. Fresh produce is affordable and abundant — mangoes, avocados, bananas, yuca, and plantains are staples. A weekly food budget for one person can range from $40 to $70 USD if you're cooking most meals. However, if you're eating out regularly at expat cafés or beachfront restaurants, expect to spend $10–$18 per meal. That said, local *sodas* (small, family-run eateries) offer generous plates of rice, beans, plantains, salad, and meat for as little as $4–$6. Learning to love *casado* — the local lunch staple — can go a long way in keeping costs manageable.

Transportation is another factor where costs can swing. If you're based in a walkable town like Puerto Viejo or Monteverde, you may not need much beyond a bicycle. But in remote areas, renting a car becomes a necessity — and that's where the budget can take a hit. Car rentals average $30–$50 per day, often more with insurance. Buying a used car is an option for long-term stays but requires navigating local bureaucracy. For most nomads, relying on public buses (cheap and surprisingly reliable) or shared shuttles between major destinations is the smarter route. Uber works well in San José and surrounding areas but hasn't officially expanded beyond the Central Valley.

Coworking memberships vary by location but are generally affordable. Expect to pay around $120–$250 per month for a dedicated desk or full-time access. Some packages include perks like fitness classes, surfboard rentals, or yoga sessions. If you only need occasional access, day passes are available at most spaces for $10–$20. Alternatively, many long-term nomads piece together a routine using coworking hubs a few times a week and home Wi-Fi the rest of the time.

Don't overlook healthcare and insurance. Costa Rica's private healthcare system is high-quality and more affordable than in many developed countries. A basic international insurance plan will cover most needs and costs around $50–$100 per month depending on age and coverage level. Local pharmacies are well-stocked, and many generic medications are available over the counter.

Finally, miscellaneous costs: SIM cards and mobile data, streaming services, fitness classes, and activities like surfing or ziplining can quietly add up. Budget at least $100–$200 per month for discretionary spending. If you're actively participating in tours, nightlife, or regular travel between towns, this number could double.

For a minimalist, locally integrated lifestyle in a smaller town, digital nomads can live comfortably on $1,200 to $1,500 per month. In contrast, those who want more privacy, amenities, and convenience — especially near beaches or in tourist-heavy hubs — should plan for $2,000 to $2,500 monthly. It's not the cheapest destination in Latin America, but Costa Rica delivers quality of life, safety, and natural beauty that justifies the spend.

Long-term digital nomads also benefit from Costa Rica's newly introduced **digital nomad visa**, which allows eligible remote workers to stay for up to a year, renewable for another year. You'll need to show proof of a consistent monthly income (around $3,000 USD) and health insurance coverage. While the process involves paperwork, it's a game-changer for those who want stability beyond the 90-day tourist visa cycle — and a major sign that Costa Rica is embracing the location-independent economy.

14.4 Community Events & Meetups

One of the quiet challenges of remote work is isolation. The Instagram version of digital nomadism rarely shows the loneliness that can creep in when you're hundreds or thousands of miles away from your support system. This is where Costa Rica shines — not just as a natural wonder, but as a place where real communities are growing and evolving.

Whether you're a developer looking for a startup meetup, a yoga teacher seeking spiritual spaces, or simply a traveler craving conversation, you'll find events and groups that welcome you in.

In Tamarindo, weekly digital nomad meetups hosted by coworking spaces like Sand & Surf often include networking mixers, tech talks, and even beach clean-up parties that blend work and purpose. Santa Teresa's creative scene thrives through collaborations: pop-up art shows, wellness circles, cacao ceremonies, and weekend DJ sets keep the community vibrant and connected. Every Thursday, a local bar may turn into a space where coders, surfers, and designers compare notes over cold beer and jungle beats.

San José, for all its concrete sprawl, hosts a surprisingly active tech and entrepreneur scene. You'll find bilingual networking nights, startup pitch competitions, and cultural exchange events coordinated by coworking giants like Impact Hub or CRHoy's event division. Language exchanges are especially popular in Heredia and Escazú, bringing together Costa Ricans eager to practice English and expats wanting to sharpen their Spanish.

Puerto Viejo, though smaller, offers soul-level community. Yoga meetups at **Om at Cashew Hill**, Afro-Caribbean cooking classes, permaculture tours, and oceanfront bonfire circles give this town a rhythm all its own. It's a favorite for creatives — not only digital nomads, but authors, musicians, and healers.

Many coliving properties now organize curated monthly calendars: workshops on conscious business, guided nature hikes, shared meals, and even mastermind sessions. Facebook groups, Telegram channels, and platforms like Meetup.com help digital nomads stay connected as they move across towns. You'll find the same faces in multiple places, forming a loose but powerful network of world travelers who've chosen Costa Rica not just for the view — but for the people they meet along the way.

Chapter 15: Family-Friendly Costa Rica

"Traveling in the company of those we love is home in motion." – Leigh Hunt

According to Costa Rica's Ministry of Tourism, over 35% of international visitors in recent years arrived as family groups — and it's easy to see why. This is not just a country that tolerates kids; it welcomes them with open arms. From its gentle beaches and interactive wildlife centers to educational eco-parks and laid-back resorts designed with families in mind, Costa Rica offers the kind of travel experience that entertains children *and* satisfies adults.

Unlike destinations where parents must constantly compromise, Costa Rica delivers a rare harmony: enough safety to inspire confidence, enough adventure to spark joy, and a national culture that genuinely values family time. Whether you're traveling with toddlers, tweens, or teens, there's something here for every age and every kind of family.

15.1 Kid-Friendly Activities by Region

In **San José and the Central Valley**, families can enjoy a soft landing into Costa Rican culture. The **Children's Museum (Museo de los Niños)** in downtown San José is more than a playhouse — it's an imaginative, hands-on exploration zone housed in a former prison. Exhibits range from space science to human anatomy, all designed with younger audiences in mind. Just outside the capital, the **Orosi Valley** offers scenic horseback riding trails that even first-time young riders can enjoy safely. Nearby, **INBioparque** (if reopened under new management) or similar nature centers offer accessible introductions to Costa Rican ecosystems.

In the **Northern Lowlands**, the town of **La Fortuna** serves as a base for families with energy to spare. Here, zip-lining companies like Ecoglide or Arenal Mundo Aventura offer tandem harnesses for small children — a thrilling but safe way for them to experience the forest canopy. The **Arenal Hot Springs**, particularly at family-oriented properties like **Baldi Hot Springs**, feature warm, shallow pools and water slides in a natural thermal setting. For kids who love critters, the **Ecocentro Danaus** and **Proyecto Asis Wildlife Rescue Center** allow up-close encounters with sloths, toucans, and howler monkeys — all while teaching animal ethics and conservation.

The **Pacific Coast**, especially **Guanacaste**, is a beach lover's paradise. The calm waters of **Playa Hermosa** or **Playa Samara** are ideal for first-time swimmers and boogie boarders. Surf schools in **Tamarindo** offer lessons specifically designed for children, with soft boards and waist-deep practice zones. In **Nicoya**, small fishing towns like **Nosara** and **Carrillo** provide peaceful, uncrowded beach days where children can build sandcastles and chase hermit crabs while parents relax under swaying palms.

On the **Caribbean Coast**, the vibe is slower, but no less captivating. In **Cahuita National Park**, a flat coastal trail runs alongside the beach, offering the rare chance to combine wildlife spotting with a dip in the sea — ideal for stroller-pushing parents or curious young hikers. The area's

Afro-Caribbean culture adds a rich dimension to the experience, with reggae rhythms, coconut rice, and a different pace of life that even children seem to adapt to effortlessly.

15.2 Wildlife Encounters & Educational Fun

For many families, wildlife is the crown jewel of a Costa Rican adventure — and it's everywhere. Sloths peer lazily from roadside trees, capuchin monkeys chatter from the canopy, and even the occasional iguana may sun itself by your hotel pool. But for a more structured encounter, Costa Rica's wildlife centers offer ethical, educational, and unforgettable experiences.

In **Monteverde**, the **Butterfly Gardens** and **Bat Jungle** are small, focused attractions perfect for short attention spans. Kids can watch butterflies emerge from chrysalises, handle harmless stick bugs, or learn how bats use echolocation — all in one afternoon.

In **Sarapiquí**, the **Tirimbina Rainforest Center** offers guided night walks, chocolate-making tours, and bridge crossings that make young explorers feel like jungle adventurers. The experience is tailored for both excitement and environmental responsibility, ensuring children don't just see nature — they begin to understand it.

Jaguar Rescue Center in **Puerto Viejo** introduces children to rescued wild animals — not as pets, but as wild beings temporarily in human care. Visitors learn about the reasons animals end up in rehabilitation and how they're prepared for release. The staff are skilled at making the information kid-friendly without dumbing it down.

In **Tortuguero**, families visiting during nesting season can witness one of nature's most moving rituals: sea turtles laying their eggs under moonlight. Strictly guided tours protect both animals and visitors, and older children in particular often describe it as a memory they'll never forget.

Meanwhile, places like **La Paz Waterfall Gardens** near **Alajuela** combine a bit of everything: waterfalls, jungle trails, big cats in spacious enclosures, and butterfly observatories — all in one neatly packaged, stroller-accessible venue.

Education is woven into these experiences naturally. Unlike static museum exhibits, Costa Rica teaches through immersion. A guide explains rainforest layers while a toucan swoops overhead. A volunteer explains turtle conservation as hatchlings wiggle toward the sea. These moments stick — not just in scrapbooks, but in young minds.

15.3 Best Family Resorts & Safe Beaches

Choosing the right home base is key when traveling with kids, and Costa Rica delivers a range of family-friendly accommodations that balance comfort, safety, and access to kid-approved activities.

In **Guanacaste**, the **Westin Reserva Conchal** is often cited as one of the best all-inclusive resorts for families. With kids' clubs, family pools, on-site naturalists, and all-you-can-eat buffets, it caters to both convenience and delight. The surrounding **Playa Conchal** is protected by a reef, creating calm waters ideal for younger swimmers.

For eco-conscious families, **Lapa Rios Lodge** on the **Osa Peninsula** offers luxury that doesn't compromise sustainability. Though more remote, it offers guided rainforest hikes suitable for children, wildlife viewing from your deck, and hands-on experiences like tortilla making or seed planting.

In **La Fortuna**, **Hotel Los Lagos** is a favorite among families thanks to its multiple hot spring pools, water slides, and easy access to Arenal Volcano and local tours. For those on a tighter budget, **Arenal Oasis Eco Lodge** provides rustic charm with forest cabins and on-site night walks led by friendly local guides.

If you're heading to the Caribbean, **Hotel Banana Azul** in **Puerto Viejo** has beachfront family suites and an easygoing atmosphere. Though the Caribbean can have stronger currents, nearby **Playa Chiquita** and **Playa Punta Uva** are known for gentle waves and warm, shallow water — perfect for safe, splash-filled afternoons.

What sets these resorts and beaches apart isn't just their amenities — it's their *approach*. Staff are accustomed to working with families. Menus cater to picky eaters. Medical services are close by, and day excursions can be adjusted for younger travelers. These places don't just allow children — they anticipate their needs, which makes all the difference.

And beyond the properties themselves, Costa Rica's cultural warmth shines through. It's common to see hotel staff crouch down to speak to children directly, to watch strangers in a restaurant gently tease a toddler, or to find a spontaneous soccer match forming on the beach. Children are welcomed, not merely accommodated.

Part 4: Practical Traveler Toolkit

Chapter 16: Budgeting & Money-Saving Tips

"Beware of little expenses. A small leak will sink a great ship."
— **Benjamin Franklin**

It's easy to fall in love with Costa Rica's wild beauty—the emerald valleys, the echo of howler monkeys at dawn, the lull of waves on Pacific beaches—but for many travelers, it's just as easy to overspend here without realizing it. What looks like a budget destination at first glance can quickly become unexpectedly expensive if you're not paying attention. The country offers incredible value—but only if you understand the hidden costs and smart spending strategies that don't make it into the glossy travel ads.

As you plan your Costa Rican journey, think of your budget not as a limitation, but as a tool for deeper, more intentional travel. Whether you're backpacking through the highlands, exploring as a couple on a romantic getaway, or managing expenses for a family trip, this chapter offers hard-earned insights that will help you spend wisely—without missing out on what matters most.

16.1 Hidden Costs to Watch

You won't find them in brochures, but hidden costs in Costa Rica can sneak up on you from the moment you land at Juan

Santamaría International Airport. These expenses aren't scams or traps—they're just part of the system, and knowing about them in advance can save you both stress and money.

Rental Cars: The Insurance Surprise

It's one of the most frequent complaints from travelers. You book a rental car online for $20 a day, thinking you've snagged a great deal—only to arrive and be told mandatory insurance will double or triple that rate. Costa Rica requires specific liability insurance that **cannot** be waived, even if you have credit card coverage. Some companies don't disclose this until pickup. Be sure to confirm the total cost in writing **before** you book. Better yet, use a reputable local company like Adobe or Vamos that clearly lists all charges upfront.

Tourist Taxes at Hotels

You might notice that the final bill for your hotel or Airbnb is higher than expected. That's because Costa Rica imposes a 13% value-added tax (VAT) on most lodging, and in many places, a 10% service fee on top of that. Even Airbnbs now charge these taxes legally. While this isn't "hidden" in a deceptive sense, it often catches travelers off guard, especially when prices are quoted in U.S. dollars without tax included.

Dining Charges You Didn't Expect

In sit-down restaurants, you'll often find a **10% service charge** added automatically to your bill. This is *not* a tip for the server—it goes to the business or shared staff pool. If your waiter gave exceptional service, a small additional tip (5–10%) is appreciated but not expected. Be aware that higher-end or touristy restaurants may also tack on a "kitchen fee" or foreign card processing surcharge. Always ask for a receipt or itemized bill.

National Park Fees for Foreigners

Costa Rica's national parks are its crown jewels, but they come at a cost. Entrance fees for foreigners often range from **$12 to $18 per person**, while locals pay far less. Some parks, like Tortuguero or Corcovado, require mandatory guides or entrance permits that add significantly to the cost. You're not being overcharged—it's a government policy that helps fund conservation—but if you plan to visit several parks, these fees add up fast. Consider purchasing multi-park passes or prioritizing free nature reserves like the **Sendero Pacifico** or **Refugio Curú**.

ATM and Currency Exchange Fees

When withdrawing cash in Costa Rica, expect fees from both your home bank and the local ATM—often totaling $6 to $10 per withdrawal. Not all ATMs offer fair exchange rates, and some charge a "convenience fee." It's smarter to withdraw larger amounts less frequently and use ATMs attached to major banks like BAC Credomatic or Banco Nacional. Also, many rural areas only accept cash, and not all vendors take dollars—so having colones on hand is essential.

Cellular Data and SIM Cards

Tourists who rely on roaming often get hit with massive phone bills after their trip. Local SIM cards are inexpensive (as low as $3) and offer generous prepaid data plans, but some providers charge activation fees or sell overpriced tourist packages at the airport. You're better off purchasing a SIM at a supermarket or kiosk in town. Kolbi (ICE), Movistar, and Claro are the major providers, each with varying coverage depending on where you go.

Transport Confusion and Added Costs

If you plan to use public buses, fares are affordable—but time delays and confusing routes can push you toward taxis or shuttles. In beach towns and tourist hubs, informal taxis (often unlicensed) may quote prices without meters and charge significantly more. Always confirm the fare upfront or use apps like **DiDi** (widely used in San José) to get fair rates. Domestic flights and ferries also charge for luggage, which isn't always disclosed during booking.

Foreign Card Surcharges & Dynamic Currency Conversion

This one catches even experienced travelers. Some businesses offer to charge your card in USD instead of colones using dynamic currency conversion (DCC). It sounds convenient, but the exchange rate is often unfavorable. Always choose to be charged in **local currency**, and double-check whether your bank charges a foreign transaction fee—some do, even for "no fee" travel cards.

16.2 Where to Eat, Stay & Play on a Budget

Costa Rica can be surprisingly gentle on the wallet—if you know where to look. The country's tourism industry has matured over the years, and while five-star eco-resorts and international dining options abound, there's still a strong culture of affordability rooted in local customs. From small, family-owned eateries to rustic but comfortable guesthouses, the real Costa Rica reveals itself not in the luxury enclaves, but in the humble, lively, and welcoming places that locals cherish and seasoned travelers return to.

Eating Well Without Spending Big

The backbone of Costa Rican dining—both culturally and economically—is the *soda*. These small, often nondescript family-run diners serve hearty portions of typical Tico food for a fraction of what you'd pay at tourist-oriented restaurants. A **casado**, the country's signature plate featuring rice, beans, salad, plantains, and your choice of protein, can cost as little as **₡2,500–₡3,500** (about $5–$7 USD), and it's both filling and flavorful. You'll often find these sodas near bus terminals, in residential areas, or even inside markets.

Street food, especially in urban centers and beach towns, is another budget-friendly gateway to the culture. Empanadas, fried plantain chips, grilled corn, and ceviche cups sold from pop-up carts or beach coolers are delicious, fast, and usually under $3. In places like Jacó, Puerto Viejo, or Tamarindo, mobile food trucks cater to both locals and backpackers, serving tacos, burritos, smoothies, and even vegan bowls for half the price of a sit-down restaurant.

When it comes to drinks, skip imported wines and international cocktails unless you're in the mood to splurge. National beers like **Imperial** and **Pilsen** are affordable and ubiquitous, often priced at $1.50–$2 in stores, slightly higher in restaurants. Many local bars also serve *guaro*—a sugarcane-based spirit—mixed into cheap but potent cocktails. Just pace yourself; the affordability can be deceiving.

For travelers staying longer or on an extremely tight budget, cooking your own meals can save a significant amount. Most hostels and budget guesthouses have shared kitchens. Supermarkets like **Pali** and **Mas x Menos** offer affordable groceries, but for the best deals and freshest produce, head to the **feria**—weekly farmers' markets held in almost every town. Prices are negotiable, and you'll get tropical fruits, vegetables, and eggs at a fraction of store prices, often directly from the grower.

Sleeping Soundly on a Shoestring

Accommodation in Costa Rica spans a wide range—from high-end resorts charging upwards of $500 per night to no-frills hostels available for less than $15. If you're budget-conscious but crave authenticity, you'll find comfort and value in **cabinas**—basic lodgings often run by locals, usually featuring private rooms, fans or A/C, and proximity to beaches or natural attractions. A clean, comfortable cabina can cost **$25–$40** per night, especially outside of peak tourist months.

Hostels have evolved significantly in Costa Rica. Many now feature private rooms alongside dorms, free Wi-Fi, surfboard rentals, tour desks, and even yoga classes or communal dinners. In beach towns like Santa Teresa or Nosara, hostels cater to both backpackers and remote workers, offering long-stay discounts and social atmospheres. The upside? You meet people, share costs, and get insider knowledge about the area.

Budget-conscious travelers looking for more privacy might consider **Airbnb**. In less tourist-saturated areas—such as Grecia, San Ramón, or Cahuita—you can often find full apartments or cabins for under $40 per night. Monthly stays sometimes include utilities and laundry, making this an excellent option for digital nomads or slow travelers.

If you're adventurous, **volunteer-based stays** (through platforms like Workaway or Worldpackers) offer room and board in exchange for a few hours of work per day—anything from teaching English to gardening at an eco-lodge. It's a great way to stretch your budget and immerse yourself in local life.

Entertainment That Doesn't Break the Bank

Costa Rica's greatest attractions are natural—and many of them are free or low-cost. Surfing at Tamarindo or Dominical? Rent a board for under $10 a day. Hiking the rainforest trails of Monteverde or La Fortuna? Many reserves offer trails for less than $5 entry, or even donation-based access if you venture off the main tourist track.

Beach days, of course, are free. So are most waterfalls, except for some that are now privatized and charge small maintenance fees (typically $2–$10). You can spend entire days swimming in rivers, watching the sunset on Playa Flamingo, or exploring tide pools in Punta Uva without spending more than a couple of dollars on snacks or transport.

Some museums in San José, like the **Museo de Arte Costarricense**, offer free entry on certain days of the week. Local cultural festivals and town celebrations—called **fiestas cívicas**—feature traditional food, music, and parades with no admission fee. Even major events like the Palmares Festival or the Limón Carnival have free concerts and community events.

Budget travelers often skip guided tours to save money, but not all tours are overpriced. In fact, many community-run co-ops offer affordable and meaningful experiences. A coffee tour in the hills outside San José might cost $15 and include tastings, a bilingual guide, and direct support to a local family business. Night walks in rainforest areas like Drake Bay—led by biologists or conservationists—are often cheaper when booked locally rather than online in advance.

The best advice? Talk to people. Locals often know of free trails, discounted boat rides, or pop-up events happening during your stay. Travelers willing to ask around and stay flexible tend to uncover the richest experiences for the smallest price tags.

16.3 Sample Daily Budgets for All Traveler Types

One of the most frequent questions asked by travelers heading to Costa Rica is also the most difficult to answer simply: "How much money will I need each day?" The truth depends on your travel style. While Costa Rica is no longer the ultra-cheap destination it once was in the backpacker trail of the 1990s, it still offers flexible price points that can suit everyone from frugal adventurers to mid-range vacationers and long-term remote workers.

Rather than offering flat numbers, this section paints realistic, scenario-based portraits of what a typical day might cost for different types of travelers in 2025–2026, taking into account food, lodging, transportation, and activities. These are not guesswork—they're based on actual rates, boots-on-the-ground habits, and local pricing trends. Keep in mind that prices vary by season, location, and personal preference, but the following breakdowns provide a strong baseline.

The Backpacker (Low Budget – $35–$55 USD per day)

The budget traveler wakes to the faint rustle of palm fronds outside a hostel dorm window in Uvita. After a cold shower and a quick chat with new friends in the common area, it's off to a local soda for a casado and coffee—$5 and filling. The day's main activity? A hike to a nearby waterfall with a $4 entry fee. No guide, no gear—just good walking shoes and a waterproof bag.

Transportation between towns is handled on public buses. A two-hour ride costs less than $5, and while it's not luxurious, it's reliable and scenic. Lunch comes from a bakery: two empanadas and a fresh juice for $3. Back at the hostel, dinner is a communal affair. Guests cook together using shared ingredients bought earlier at the feria for a total of $4 per person. A local beer on the rooftop terrace costs $1.50. After that, maybe some live music at a free event in town or a swim in the hostel's pool. The room for the night? A dorm bed at $12.

For this traveler, comfort is basic, but the experience is rich—and the cost is consistently manageable with smart choices.

The Mid-Range Explorer (Comfort Budget – $90–$130 USD per day)

This traveler values convenience, privacy, and curated experiences. In La Fortuna, they wake in a modest but stylish guesthouse with a private room, hot water, and A/C—around $50 a night, breakfast included. The morning is spent soaking in nearby hot springs (entry: $18), followed by a guided nature walk with a certified guide at a biological reserve ($25).

Lunch is a sit-down meal at a scenic cafe with a mountain view. A fresh grilled tilapia plate and smoothie costs about $12. After a relaxed afternoon nap, the traveler ventures into town for dinner at a well-reviewed fusion spot. Three courses and a local craft beer set them back $22. Transport includes occasional short rides with DiDi or a shared shuttle if covering longer distances.

This kind of travel isn't extravagant, but it's comfortable, easy, and focused on maximizing experience per dollar. These travelers often leave Costa Rica feeling satisfied—not because they didn't spend, but because they spent smart.

The Digital Nomad (Slow Travel Budget – $50–$85 USD per day)

The digital nomad rents a furnished studio apartment in San Ramón for $600/month, bringing their daily accommodation cost down to $20. High-speed fiber internet is included, and the building has shared laundry facilities. A coworking space is nearby, but they often work from a cafe with strong Wi-Fi and good coffee. A double espresso and pastry costs $4.

Groceries are purchased weekly—mostly local produce, rice, beans, chicken, and fruit—keeping food costs around $10–$15 per day. Eating out happens 2–3 times a week at local sodas or international kitchens popular with expats.

Because of the slower pace, the nomad doesn't tour constantly but takes weekend trips: a beach visit here, a volcano hike there. These are budgeted in, spread over the month. Daily transportation is minimal—maybe a $1 bus fare or $3 taxi. Their lifestyle balances productivity and adventure without burning through savings. Flexibility is their most valuable currency.

The Traveling Family (Moderate Budget – $150–$250 USD per day)

A family of four lands in Costa Rica with a strong emphasis on comfort, safety, and ease. They rent a mid-range hotel or family Airbnb near Playa Hermosa for $120 a night. The unit has a kitchen, allowing them to cook breakfasts and occasional dinners—keeping costs manageable.

A typical day includes a guided wildlife boat tour through the mangroves ($35 per adult, $20 per child), followed by lunch at a beachfront restaurant ($45 total with drinks and kids' meals). Ice cream or fresh fruit smoothies are a daily treat ($8). Local transport is done via rental car, which adds about $50/day including fuel. This gives the family the freedom to explore nearby towns, waterfalls, and less-accessible beaches.

Dinner is out, usually at casual restaurants with kids' menus. Total cost: $50–$60 depending on location. Despite the higher daily expenses, the family values safety, ease of movement, and quality experiences tailored to young travelers—and Costa Rica delivers on all fronts.

Across all categories, the takeaway is simple: **Costa Rica rewards those who do their homework**. Whether you're spending $35 or $200 a day, smart choices—local food, public transportation, off-season travel, and authentic lodging—unlock better value without compromising experience.

In the end, the real luxury in Costa Rica isn't about five-star hotels or helicopter rides. It's about waking up to the sound of toucans, swimming in rivers with no one else around, and knowing that every dollar you spent helped you feel more alive, more connected, and more curious about the world.

Chapter 17: Health, Safety & Travel Insurance

17.1 Common Illnesses & How to Avoid Them

"In Costa Rica, a paradise of waterfalls and volcanoes, the most common thing you'll bring home isn't a scar or a story—it's a mild stomach bug."

While Costa Rica is considered one of the safest and most well-developed countries in Central America, the tropical climate and different standards of hygiene can expose travelers to health concerns unfamiliar to those from North America or Europe. The good news is that most of these issues are preventable with preparation and awareness.

The most frequently encountered illness among travelers is **traveler's diarrhea**. Caused by unfamiliar bacteria in food or water, it's not a reflection of how "dirty" a place is—often, it's just your body reacting to new microbes. Tap water in most parts of Costa Rica is technically potable, especially in cities like San José, Liberia, and tourist-developed zones like La Fortuna or Tamarindo. However, in rural areas or along the Caribbean coast, it's safer to stick to bottled or filtered water. That includes when brushing your teeth or making ice.

Avoiding raw foods—like salads washed in untreated water—or street food that's been sitting out uncovered for hours, can reduce the chance of infection. Opt for busy food stands with high turnover and freshly cooked meals. If you do end up with stomach issues, hydration is key. Pharmacies (farmacias) are widely available, and the local go-to remedy for upset stomach is "Suero Oral" (oral rehydration solution), which you can buy over the counter.

Next on the list are **mosquito-borne illnesses**, including dengue fever, chikungunya, and to a lesser extent, Zika virus. These are more common in the wet season, particularly in lowland and coastal areas like Limón or the Osa Peninsula. While malaria is not a major concern in Costa Rica, dengue fever is. Unlike malaria-carrying mosquitoes, dengue mosquitoes bite during the day, so travelers shouldn't let their guard down outside of evening hours. The best defense is insect repellent with DEET (at least 20–30%), wearing long sleeves and pants in dense vegetation or jungle areas, and sleeping in rooms with good screens or mosquito nets. A travel-size plug-in mosquito repeller can also be a smart packing addition.

Heat-related illnesses are often underestimated by travelers coming from cooler climates. With year-round temperatures in the 80s or higher and humidity levels that can hover around 90% in the jungle, dehydration can sneak up on even experienced hikers or beachgoers. Electrolyte packets or local hydration drinks like "Agua de Pipa" (fresh coconut water) are widely available and effective. Always carry a refillable water bottle—Costa Rica has many public fountains and refill stations in eco-conscious hotels and hostels.

Sunburn is another surprisingly common ailment, especially among those who spend time in the highland areas or at the beach. The UV index in Costa Rica is consistently high due to its proximity to the equator. Even on overcast days, unprotected skin can burn in under 30 minutes. Sunscreen is available locally, but it's often expensive and not always reef-safe, which is a concern in areas like Cahuita or the Nicoya Peninsula, where coral reefs are present. Bring a reef-friendly SPF 30+ sunscreen from home if you're planning beach or water activities.

Another issue worth noting is **allergies**—not from food necessarily, but from insect bites, pollen, and jungle plants. Some travelers have allergic reactions to ant or mosquito bites that require antihistamines, which are easy to purchase in Costa Rican pharmacies without a prescription. If you have severe allergies or carry an EpiPen, always keep it on you, especially if you're venturing into remote national parks or forests where help is not immediately accessible.

Lastly, **animal-related injuries**, though rare, do occur. Monkey bites, for example, are a growing issue in some tourist-heavy areas like Manuel Antonio where visitors feed wildlife against park rules. It's not just discouraged—it's dangerous. Wild animals may carry bacteria or parasites that can result in infection or disease. Do not touch or feed monkeys, sloths, raccoons, or even domestic dogs unless you are with a guide or at a trusted rescue facility. If bitten or scratched, clean the wound immediately and seek medical attention.

Costa Rica's medical system is one of the best in Latin America. The public system (Caja Costarricense de Seguro Social, or CCSS) is reliable, and the private sector offers high-quality care at affordable prices. Major cities have modern hospitals, and even remote towns will usually have a small clinic. Pharmacies are staffed with trained professionals who can often prescribe basic medication without a doctor's visit. Still, it's smart to bring a small travel medical kit with basics like painkillers, antihistamines, Imodium, anti-itch cream, and band-aids.

Whether you're hiking a volcano, surfing in Tamarindo, or lounging in a jungle lodge, the best way to stay healthy in Costa Rica is a combination of **preparation, observation, and respect**—for your body and for the environment you're exploring.

17.2 Staying Safe in Urban vs Rural Areas

Costa Rica is generally safe for travelers, but the experience of safety can differ sharply between its urban and rural settings. Knowing what to expect—and how to adapt—can be the difference between a stress-free trip and an unfortunate incident.

In cities like San José, Heredia, or Limón, **petty crime** is the most common threat to travelers. Pickpocketing, bag-snatching, and opportunistic theft can occur in crowded places such as bus terminals, downtown markets, or poorly lit neighborhoods. Travelers should avoid walking alone at night in unfamiliar areas, keep valuables close to the body (not in back pockets or loose bags), and avoid flashing expensive electronics or jewelry. Ubers and licensed taxis are safer options than flagging down cabs on the street.

Urban scams do exist, especially in San José. A common tactic involves someone "helping" with directions or offering unsolicited tour advice, only to ask for money or lead the traveler somewhere unsafe. While Costa Ricans (Ticos) are famously friendly, use the same street-smarts you'd apply in any unfamiliar city. If you're approached by someone overly eager, trust your instincts.

Public parks, particularly at night, should be avoided unless they are well-lit and active with other visitors. Despite the romantic image of wandering through the city's historical districts or plazas after dark, it's better to plan nightlife around known venues or guided events. Most hotels offer vetted recommendations and even transport arrangements.

In contrast, **rural areas** tend to feel much safer, especially in smaller towns like Monteverde, Santa Elena, or Puerto Viejo de Talamanca. Crime rates are generally lower, and the atmosphere is more relaxed. That said, complacency can also be a risk. The remoteness of some villages means that emergency services might be far away, and travelers engaging in solo hiking or off-road exploration should always inform someone of their plans and expected return time.

While violent crime is rare in tourist areas, theft still happens. In beach towns, it's common for rental cars to be broken into, especially if bags are left visible. Always keep valuables out of sight or better yet, take them with you. Use hotel safes when available, and avoid bringing irreplaceable items unless absolutely necessary.

Natural hazards also differ between urban and rural areas. In cities, you're more likely to face manmade dangers—reckless driving, unmarked construction, or outdated infrastructure. In rural zones, **natural threats** such as flash flooding, rough hiking trails, or unexpected encounters with wildlife are more common. Tourists have been injured attempting to swim in unauthorized rivers or climb waterfalls without proper gear. These aren't theme parks—nature here is wild and unpredictable.

Police presence is more visible in urban areas, particularly around San José and airports. In rural areas, the **Tourist Police** (Policía Turística) may be available in hotspots like Manuel Antonio or Tamarindo. They are trained to assist international visitors and usually speak basic English.

Ultimately, Costa Rica rewards the respectful and the prepared. Urban and rural settings each offer their own kind of adventure, but the smartest travelers are the ones who observe, adapt, and move confidently without letting their guard down entirely.

Chapter 18: Spanish Phrases for Travelers

"You can never understand one language until you understand at least two." — *Geoffrey Willans*

In Costa Rica, English can take you pretty far in the touristy zones—hotels, airports, and many tour agencies speak it with ease. But outside those bubbles, the moment you walk into a small local *soda* (a casual eatery), flag down a taxi, or wander through a hillside village, you'll quickly realize that even a small Spanish vocabulary can open doors. More than that, it earns respect. Ticos (Costa Ricans) don't expect you to be fluent, but they deeply appreciate the effort. A single "gracias" delivered with warmth can soften even the most hurried shopkeeper.

Spanish here is simple, melodic, and often softened by the Costa Rican personality—humble, friendly, non-confrontational. That said, pronunciation does matter, and word choice, especially with Tico slang, can make all the difference between sounding like a clumsy tourist or a well-meaning visitor.

18.1 Essential Words & Phrases

Start with the basics. These are not just vocabulary items; they are your social passport. Words like *hola* (hello), *por favor* (please), and *gracias* (thank you) may seem obvious, but when said with eye contact and a smile, they transform the energy of any interaction. It's not just about saying the right thing; it's about showing you care enough to try.

When asking for help, *¿Dónde está...?* (Where is...?) is your Swiss army knife. Whether it's a restroom (*el baño*), an ATM (*el cajero*), or a bus stop (*la parada de autobús*), this phrase will be your starting point.

One phrase many overlook is *Disculpe* (Excuse me), which is useful in crowded markets, when trying to get someone's attention, or even just as a polite entry into a question. It's more refined than *perdón* and less abrupt than just calling out.

And when things go wrong—as they sometimes do—*No entiendo* (I don't understand) and *¿Puede repetir, por favor?* (Can you repeat, please?) are your best defenses. Polite confusion is better than pretending to follow along and ending up on a bus bound for the wrong province.

Then there's *¿Cuánto cuesta?* (How much does it cost?), which is indispensable whether you're bargaining at a beachside souvenir stand or checking prices at a roadside fruit stall. Ticos rarely overcharge, but it helps to ask with confidence.

18.2 Restaurant, Market, & Taxi Language

In a local eatery, the dance of ordering food is a ritual of its own. If the menu is in Spanish, don't panic. Most dishes come with simple, recognizable names: *arroz con pollo* (rice with chicken), *casado* (a traditional plate often with rice, beans, meat, plantains, and salad), or *gallo pinto* (a breakfast staple of rice and beans).

When you're ready to order, simply say: *Quisiera...* (I would like...). This is gentler than the more direct *quiero* and considered more polite. So instead of barking *"quiero una cerveza,"* try *"Quisiera una cerveza, por favor."* You'll instantly sound more respectful—and less like you're at a frat party.

In markets, numbers matter. While many vendors hold up fingers or punch amounts into calculators, it still helps to recognize *mil* (thousand), *quinientos* (five hundred), and *cien* (one hundred). Costa Rican currency uses colones, and prices often run high in numerical value. A bottle of water might be 800 colones, while a T-shirt might be 5000. Hearing "cinco mil" (five thousand) doesn't mean you're being scammed—it's just how the money works.

In taxis, always greet the driver and confirm that the meter (*el taxímetro*) is running. Ask: *¿Puede poner el taxímetro, por favor?* It signals that you know the system. While most city taxis are honest, the occasional opportunist might "forget" to switch it on unless prompted.

When giving directions or asking to be dropped somewhere, simplicity helps. Try: *Voy al hotel [name]* (I'm going to Hotel [name]) or *¿Puede llevarme al centro?* (Can you take me to downtown?). Even if you mispronounce, they'll usually figure it out.

18.3 Fun Local Slang (Tico-isms!)

And then there's *Tico talk*. Costa Ricans don't just speak Spanish—they personalize it. Their Spanish is peppered with idioms, local expressions, and playful turns of phrase that can confuse even advanced learners. But once you get the hang of a few, you'll not only understand more—you'll feel more *in* Costa Rica.

The most famous phrase is *¡Pura vida!* It means everything and nothing. It's hello, goodbye, thank you, I'm good, life is beautiful, and stop worrying. It's less a phrase and more a way of being. Say it with a smile, and you're in.

Another word you'll hear constantly is *Tico* (male) or *Tica* (female). These are affectionate terms Costa Ricans use for themselves. So if someone says, *"Soy Tica,"* they're telling you they're a proud Costa Rican woman.

Then there's *mae*—pronounced like "my." It's the Tico version of "dude" or "bro," used informally among friends. You'll hear it mostly among the younger crowd: *"Mae, ese lugar está tuanis."* (Dude, that place is awesome.)

Speaking of *tuanis*, it's one of the weirdest and most beloved slang terms in the country. It means cool, great, awesome. No one's quite sure where it came from—some say it's a distortion of the English phrase "too nice"—but regardless, it's everywhere. A beach sunset is *tuanis*. A great meal is *tuanis*. A new friend who shares their local tips is definitely *tuanis*.

Feeling tired? You might say *estoy hecho leña*—literally "I'm made of firewood," but in practice, it means "I'm wiped out." It's a colorful way to say you're beat, and it earns a grin from anyone local who hears it.

Want to sound extra local? Try *diay*—a word that means nothing and everything. It's a filler, like "well" or "so," and often starts sentences: *"Diay, vamos a la playa, ¿no?"* It's casual, fun, and pure Costa Rican rhythm.

Map

Printed in Dunstable, United Kingdom

66272220R00121